Model Year 2014

Fuel Economy Guide

I0436052

www.fueleconomy.gov

fueleconomy.gov/m for your mobile device

U.S. Department of Energy
Office of Energy Efficiency and Renewable Energy
U.S. Environmental Protection Agency
UPDATED: February 28, 2014

U.S. DEPARTMENT OF
ENERGY
DOE/EE-0957

EPA

Model Year 2014
Fuel Economy Guide

www.fueleconomy.gov

contents

USING THE *FUEL ECONOMY GUIDE*

The U.S. Environmental Protection Agency (EPA) and U.S. Department of Energy (DOE) produce the *Fuel Economy Guide* to help car buyers choose the most fuel-efficient vehicle that meets their needs. The Guide is published in print and on the Web at **www.fueleconomy. gov**. For additional print copies, mail your request to: NREL - Fuel Economy Guide, 15013 Denver West Parkway, Golden, CO 80401-3305, or enter your request electronically at **http://www. fueleconomy.gov/feg/contacts.shtml.**

Fuel Economy Estimates

Most vehicles in this Guide (other than plug-in hybrids) have three fuel economy estimates:

- A "city" estimate that represents urban driving, in which a vehicle is started in the morning (after being parked all night) and driven in stop-and-go traffic
- A "highway" estimate that represents a mixture of rural and interstate highway driving in a warmed-up vehicle, typical of longer trips in free-flowing traffic
- A "combined" estimate that represents a combination of city driving (55%) and highway driving (45%)

Estimates for all vehicles are based on laboratory testing under standardized conditions to allow for fair comparisons.

Flexible-fuel vehicles (FFVs), which can use gasoline and E85, have estimates for both fuels. Plug-in hybrid electric vehicles (PHEVs) have estimates for (1) electric-only or blended electric and gasoline operation and (2) gasoline-only operation. PHEVs are discussed in more detail on page 32. For answers to frequently asked questions about fuel economy estimates, visit **www.fueleconomy.gov**.

Annual Fuel Cost Estimates

This Guide provides annual fuel cost estimates, rounded to the nearest $50, for each vehicle.. The estimates are based on the assumptions that you travel 15,000 miles per year (55% under city driving conditions and 45% under highway conditions) and that fuel costs $3.44/gallon for regular unleaded gasoline and $3.78/gallon for premium. Cost-per-gallon assumptions for vehicles that use other fuel types are discussed at the beginning of those vehicle sections. The fuel costs were determined in advance to allow time for printing fuel economy labels; thus the Guide may not reflect current fuel prices.

Visit **www.fueleconomy.gov** to personalize fuel costs based on current fuel prices and your driving habits.

Your Fuel Economy Will Vary

Even though EPA recently improved its methods for estimating fuel economy, your vehicle's fuel economy will almost certainly vary from EPA's estimate. Fuel economy is not a fixed number; it varies significantly based on where you drive, how you drive, and other factors. Thus, it is impossible for one set of estimates to predict fuel economy precisely for all drivers in all environments. For example, the following factors can lower your vehicle's fuel economy:

- Aggressive driving (hard acceleration and braking)
- Excessive idling, accelerating, and braking in stop-and-go traffic
- Cold weather (engines are more efficient when warmed up)
- Driving with a heavy load or with the air conditioner running
- Improperly tuned engine or under-inflated tires
- Use of remote starters

In addition, small variations in vehicle manufacturing can cause fuel economy variations in the same make and model, and some vehicles don't attain maximum fuel economy until they are "broken in" (around 3,000–5,000 miles).

So, please remember that the EPA ratings are a useful tool for comparing vehicles when car buying, but they may not accurately predict the fuel economy you will get. This is also true for annual fuel cost estimates. For more information on fuel economy ratings and factors that affect fuel economy, visit **www.fueleconomy.gov**.

UNDERSTANDING THE GUIDE LISTINGS

We hope you'll find the *Fuel Economy Guide* easy to use! Fuel economy and annual fuel cost data are organized by vehicle class (see page 2 for a list of classes). Within each class, vehicles are listed alphabetically by manufacturer and model.

Vehicle models with different features, such as engine size or transmission type, are listed as different vehicles. Engine and transmission attributes are shown in the first column under the model name.

Additional attributes needed to distinguish among vehicles (e.g., fuel type or suggested fuel grade) are listed in the "Notes" column. A legend for abbreviations is provided on page 6.

A "P" in the "Notes" column indicates that the manufacturer *recommends* that the vehicle be fueled with premium-grade gasoline, and a "PR" indicates that the manufacturer *requires* premium. The higher price of premium fuel is reflected in the annual fuel cost for these vehicles.

The most fuel-efficient vehicles in each class and alternative fuel vehicles are indicated with special markings (see diagram below). Vehicles that can use more than one kind of fuel have an entry for each fuel type.

Interior passenger and cargo volumes are located in the index at the back of the Guide.

WHY SOME VEHICLES ARE NOT LISTED

Light-duty fuel economy regulations do not apply to

* Sport utility vehicles (SUVs) and passenger vans with a gross vehicle weight rating (GVWR) of more than 10,000 pounds—GVWR is the vehicle weight plus carrying capacity

* Other vehicles with a GVWR of 8,500 pounds or more or a curb weight over 6,000 pounds

Therefore, manufacturers do not have to estimate their fuel economy, and fuel economy labels are not posted on their windows..

Also, fuel economy information on some vehicles is not available in time to be printed in the Guide. However, you can find more up-to-date information at www.fueleconomy.gov.

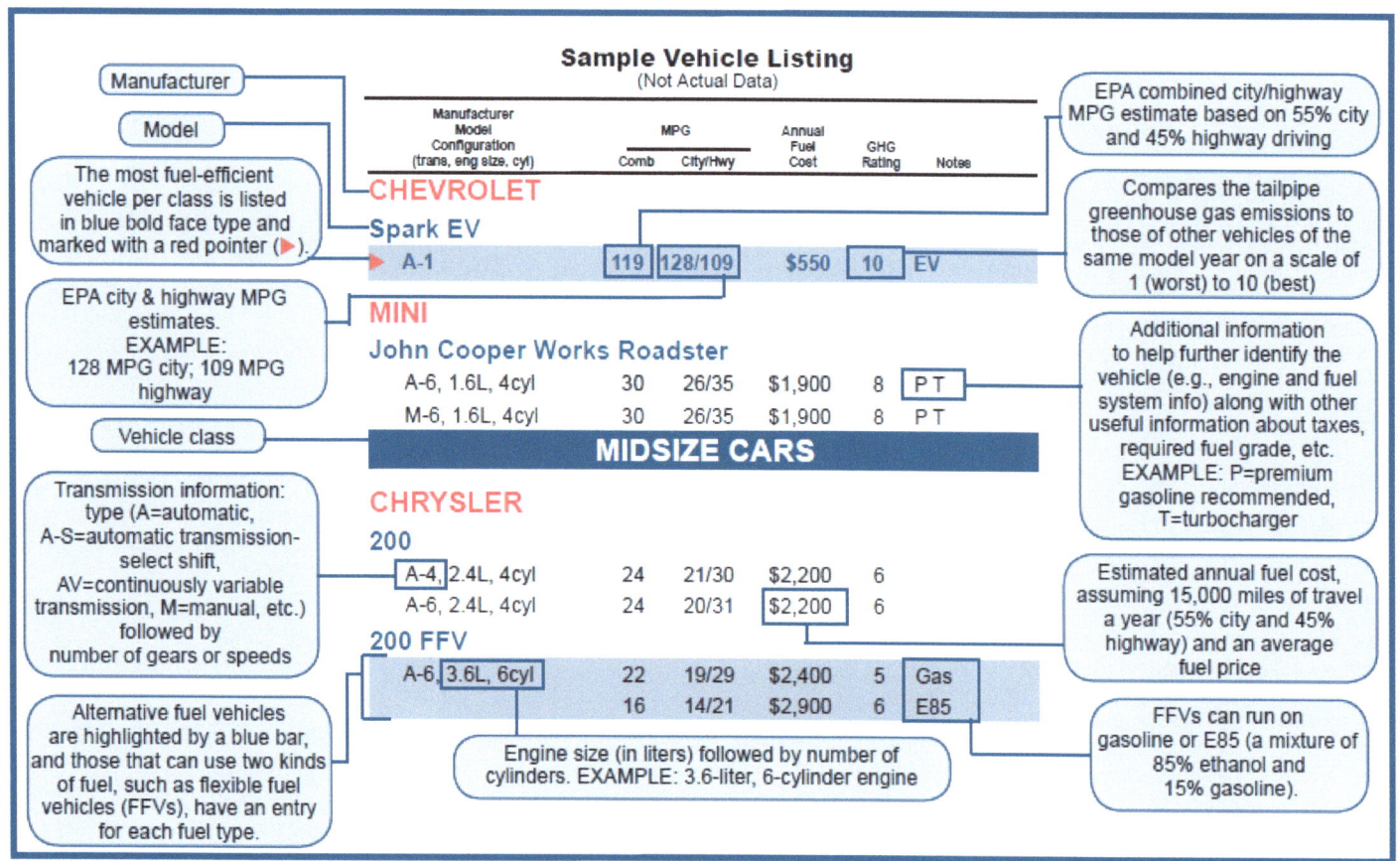

VEHICLE CLASSES USED IN THIS GUIDE

	CARS		TRUCKS	
	Passenger and Cargo			**Gross Vehicle**
CLASS	**Volume** (cu. ft.)	**CLASS**		**Weight Rating*** (pounds)
TWO-SEATERS		**PICKUP TRUCKS**		
SEDANS		Small		Under 6,000
Minicompact	Under 85	Standard		6,000 to 8,500
Subcompact	85 to 99	**VANS**		
Compact	100 to 109	Passenger		Under 10,000
Midsize	110 to 119	Cargo		Under 8,500
Large	120 or more	**MINIVANS**		Under 8,500
STATION WAGONS		**SPORT UTILITY VEHICLES**		
Small	Under 130	Small		Under 6,000
Midsize	130 to 159	Standard		6,000 to 9.999
Large	160 or more	**SPECIAL PURPOSE VEHICLES**		Under 8,500

*Gross Vehicle Weight Rating = vehicle weight plus carrying capacity.

TAX INCENTIVES AND DISINCENTIVES

Federal Tax Credits

You may be eligible for a federal income tax credit of up to $7,500 if you purchase a qualifying electric or plug-in hybrid vehicle in 2013–14.

Visit www.fueleconomy.gov for more information on qualifying models, credit amounts, and phase-out dates.

Gas Guzzler Tax

The Energy Tax Act of 1978 requires auto companies to pay a "gas guzzler" tax on the sale of cars with exceptionally low fuel economy. Such vehicles are identified in the Guide by the word "Tax" in the "Notes" column. In the dealer showroom, the words "Gas Guzzler" and the tax amount are listed on the vehicle's fuel economy label. The tax does not apply to light trucks.

WHY CONSIDER FUEL ECONOMY?

Save Money

You could save as much as $1,700 in fuel costs each year by choosing the most fuel-efficient vehicle in a particular class. This can add up to thousands of dollars over a vehicle's lifetime. Fuel-efficient models come in all shapes and sizes, so you need not sacrifice utility or size.

Each vehicle listing in the *Fuel Economy Guide* provides an estimated annual fuel cost (see page i). The Find and Compare Cars tool at www.fueleconomy.gov features an annual fuel cost calculator that allows you to insert your local gasoline prices and typical driving conditions (percentage of city and highway driving) to obtain the most accurate fuel cost information for your vehicle.

Reduce Oil Dependence Costs

Buying a more fuel-efficient vehicle can help reduce our dependence on petroleum. Nearly 40% of the oil used to produce the gasoline you put in your tank is imported. The United States uses about 19 million barrels of oil per day, two-thirds of which is used for transportation. Oil dependence cost the U.S. economy around $500 billion in 2012 alone.

Reduce Climate Change

Climate change is widely viewed as the most significant long-term threat to the global environment, and human-made emissions of greenhouse gases (GHGs) are very likely the cause of most of the observed global warming over the last 50 years.

Burning fossil fuels such as gasoline and diesel releases carbon dioxide (CO_2) and other GHGs into the atmosphere, contributing to global climate change. CO_2 is the most important human-made GHG, and highway vehicles account for almost a quarter (1.7 billion tons) of U.S. CO_2 emissions each year.

Every gallon of gasoline your vehicle burns puts about 20 pounds of CO_2 into the atmosphere; the average vehicle emits around 5 to 8 tons of CO_2 each year. Unlike other forms of vehicle pollution, CO_2 emissions cannot be reduced by pollution control technologies. They can only be reduced by burning less fuel or by burning fuel that contains less carbon.

One of the most important things you can do to reduce your contribution to climate change is to buy a vehicle with better fuel economy. Switching from a vehicle that gets 20 miles per gallon (MPG) to one that gets 25 MPG can reduce CO_2 emissions by 10 tons over a vehicle's lifetime, more than a year's worth of use.

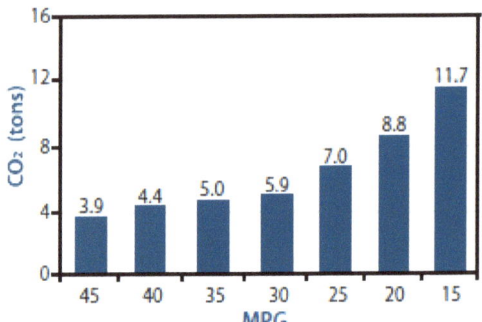

Annual CO₂ Emissions by Vehicle MPG

You can also reduce your contribution to climate change by

- Getting the best fuel economy out of your car

- Using a low-carbon fuel, such as compressed natural gas (CNG) or electricity from a renewable resource such as wind or hydropower

- Walking, biking, or taking public transit more often

FUELING OPTIONS

Ethanol Blends – E85 & E10

Ethanol is a domestically produced, renewable fuel made primarily from starch-based crops such as corn. It may also be made from "cellulosic biomass," such as crop residues and wood, but this is not yet done on a large scale. The use of ethanol as a vehicle fuel can reduce GHG emissions and U.S. dependence on

petroleum.

E10 is a blend of 10% ethanol and 90% gasoline and is legal for use in any gasoline-powered vehicle. More than 95% of U.S. gasoline contains up to 10% ethanol to boost octane, meet air quality requirements, or satisfy the federal Renewable Fuel Standard.

E85 is a high-level ethanol-gasoline blend containing 51% to 83% ethanol, depending on the season and geographic location. Drivers can use E85 in flexible fuel vehicles (FFVs), which are specially designed to run on gasoline, E85, or any mixture of the two. FFVs are offered by several vehicle manufacturers. To determine whether your vehicle is an FFV, check the inside of your car's fuel filler door for an identification sticker or consult your owner's manual. More than 2,300 filling stations in the United States currently sell E85. Visit afdc.energy.gov/locator/stations/ to find stations near you.

There is no noticeable difference in vehicle performance when low-level ethanol blends are used. However, FFVs operating on E85 usually experience a 25–30% drop in fuel economy due to ethanol's lower energy content relative to gasoline.

Biodiesel

Biodiesel is a domestically produced renewable fuel manufactured from vegetable oils or animal fats for use in diesel vehicles. Using biodiesel in place of petroleum diesel reduces greenhouse gas emissions and contributes to national energy security.

Biodiesel can be blended with petroleum diesel at any percentage. The most common biodiesel blend is B20, which contains 20% biodiesel and 80% petroleum diesel. B5 (5% biodiesel and 95% petroleum diesel) is another common blend. All vehicle manufacturers have approved biodiesel blends up to and including B5 for use in all diesel engines. However, using higher-level biodiesel blends may affect vehicle warranties.

Check your owner's manual or with your vehicle manufacturer to determine the right blend for your vehicle.

Purchase commercial-grade biodiesel from a reputable dealer. Never refuel with recycled grease or vegetable oil that has not been converted to biodiesel. It will damage your engine.

More than 300 stations currently dispense B20. Visit afdc.energy.gov/afdc/locator/stations to find service stations selling biodiesel near you.

Premium- vs. Regular-Grade Gasoline

Regular unleaded is the recommended gasoline for most cars. Using a higher-octane gasoline than recommended by the owner's manual does not improve performance or fuel efficiency; it only costs more money. Check your owner's manual to determine the lowest grade of fuel you can use.

FUEL ECONOMY AND ANNUAL FUEL COST RANGES FOR VEHICLE CLASSES

The graph below provides the fuel economy and annual fuel cost ranges for the vehicles in each class so you can see where a given vehicle's fuel economy and cost fall within its class. Combined city and highway MPG estimates are used; these assume you will drive 55% in the city and 45% on the highway. Annual fuel costs assume you travel 15,000 miles each year and fuel costs $3.44/gallon for regular unleaded gasoline and $3.78/gallon for premium, $4.02 for diesel, and $.12/kWh for electricity. Visit www.fueleconomy.gov to calculate annual fuel cost for a specific vehicle based on your own driving conditions and fuel prices.

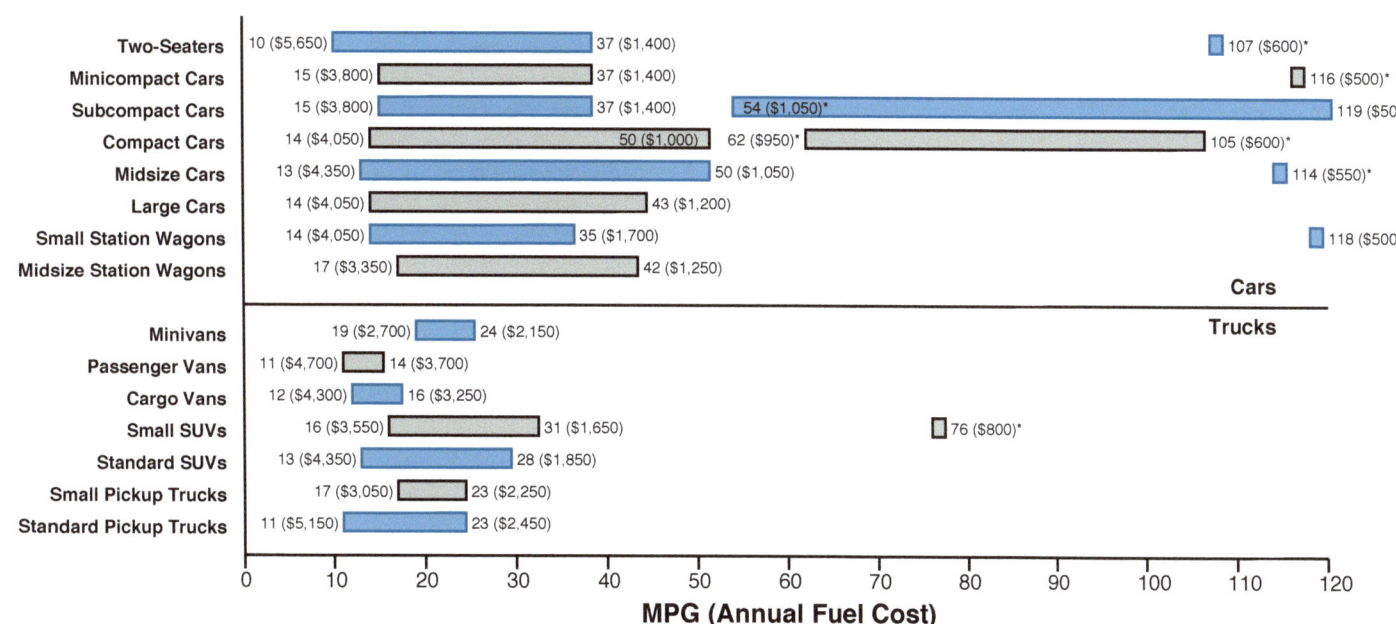

Fuel economy estimates on this chart do not include vehicles operating on compressed natural gas (CNG), hydrogen, or E85.
* Represents electric vehicles and plug-in hybrids. Fuel economy values for these vehicles are in miles per gallon gasoline equivalent (MPGe).

FUEL-SAVING TECHNOLOGY HIGHLIGHT: START-STOP SYSTEMS

An energy-saving feature is now available that can help you save fuel in stop-and-go traffic, at red lights, and in other situations where your car would normally waste fuel idling. Start-stop systems—also called idle-stop, smart start, or other manufacturer-specifi c names—turn off the engine when a vehicle comes to a stop and automatically start it back up when the brake is released or when the accelerator or clutch is pressed. It usually takes half a second or less to restart.

Until recently, these systems were mostly found on hybrid vehicles, but as of the 2014 model year, they are available on about one hundred conventional vehicle models.

By turning off the engine when it's not needed, start-stop systems can improve fuel economy by around 4 to 5 percent on average—less in highway driving or when the air conditioning is in heavy use. Unlike a hybrid system, which can add thousands of dollars to a vehicle's cost, a start-stop system typically adds only a few hundred dollars.

Starting and stopping the engine more often won't increase wear on the engine, and these systems are equipped with special starters, batteries, and alternators built to handle the increased performance requirements.

Since heating, air conditioning, and other cabin accessories are usually powered by the engine, these systems are designed to maintain and/or manage power for those accessories when the engine is stopped. For example, some vehicles restart the engine when the cabin temperature changes or when the battery charge is low.

A start-stop system doesn't require you to drive differently, but it may take some time for you to get used to the way the vehicle operates or feels. Most systems are robust and easy to use.

While the concept is straightforward, there are differences in the way start-stop systems on different vehicles operate, perform, and manage power for accessories. If you spend significant drive time idling, a vehicle equipped with a start-stop system might just be right for you!

IMPROVE YOUR FUEL ECONOMY

Drive More Efficiently

- Aggressive driving (speeding and rapid acceleration/braking) can lower your gas mileage by as much as 33% at highway speeds and 5% around town.

- Observe the speed limit. Each 5 MPH you drive over 60 MPH can reduce your fuel economy by 7%.

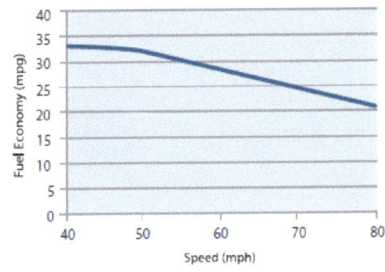

- Avoid idling. Idling gets 0 miles per gallon and costs as much as $0.04 per minute.

- Using cruise control on the highway helps you maintain a constant speed and, in most cases, will save gas.

Keep Your Car in Shape

- Fixing a car that is noticeably out of tune can improve gas mileage your gas mileage by about 4%.

- Keeping tires inflated to the recommended pressure and using the recommended grade of motor oil can improve fuel economy by up to 5%.

  The manufacturer's recommended tire pressure can be found on the tire information placard and/or vehicle certification label located on the vehicle door edge, doorpost, glove-box door, or inside the trunk lid.

- Keep your tires aligned and balanced.

- Replacing a clogged air filter can improve gas mileageon older cars with carbureted engines.

Plan and Combine Trips

- A warmed-up engine is more fuel-efficient than a cold one. Many short trips taken from a cold start can use twice as much fuel as one multipurpose trip covering the same distance.

Note: Letting your car idle to warm up doesn't help your fuel economy, it actually uses more fuel and creates more pollution.

Other Solutions

- Avoid carrying unneeded items. An extra 100 pounds can decrease fuel economy by 1%-2%.

- A roof rack or carrier provides additional cargo space and may allow you to meet your needs with a smaller car. However, a loaded roof rack can decrease your fuel economy by 5%.

  Reduce aerodynamic drag and improve your fuel economy by placing items inside the trunk whenever possible.

For more mileage tips and information about gasoline pricing, visit www.fueleconomy.gov.

MODEL YEAR 2014 FUEL ECONOMY LEADERS

Listed below are vehicles with the highest fuel economy in the most popular classes. For each vehicle class, we list the most fuel-efficient plug-in hybrid or electric (EV) and the most fuel-efficient conventional vehicle. Rankings are based on combined city and highway fuel economy estimates which assume 55% city driving and 45% highway driving. Please note that many vehicle models come in a range of engine sizes and trim lines, resulting in different fuel economy values. If there is only one vehicle in the class, we do not list a fuel economy leader.

	Trans Type/ Speeds	Eng Size / Cylinders	MPG Combined
TWO-SEATER CARS			
SMART			
fortwo electric drive convertible	A-1		107*
fortwo electric drive coupe	A-1		107*
HONDA			
CR-Z	AV-S7	1.5/4	37
MINICOMPACT CARS			
FIAT			
500e	A-1		116*
SCION			
iQ	AV	1.3/4	37
SUBCOMPACT CARS			
CHEVROLET			
Spark EV	A-1		119*
FORD			
Fiesta SFE FWD	M-5	1.0/3	37
COMPACT CARS			
FORD			
Focus Electric	A-1		105*
TOYOTA			
Prius c	AV	1.5/4	50
MIDSIZE CARS			
NISSAN			
Leaf	A-1		114*
FORD			
C-MAX Energi Plug-in Hybrid	AV	2.0/4	58†
Fusion Energi Plug-in Hybrid	AV	2.0/4	58†
TOYOTA			
Prius Plug-in Hybrid	AV	1.8/4	58†
Prius	AV	1.8/4	50
LARGE CARS			
FORD			
C-MAX Hybrid FWD	AV	2.0/4	43
SMALL STATION WAGONS			
HONDA			
Fit EV	A-1		118*
BMW			
328d xDrive Sports Wagon (diesel)	A-S8	2.0/4	35
MIDSIZE STATION WAGONS			
TOYOTA			
Prius v	AV	1.8/4	42

	Trans Type/ Speeds	Eng Size / Cylinders	MPG Combined
SMALL PICKUP TRUCKS			
TOYOTA			
Tacoma 2WD	M-5	2.7/4	23
STANDARD PICKUP TRUCKS			
RAM			
1500 2WD (diesel)	A-8	3.0/6	23
VANS, CARGO			
CHEVROLET			
Express 1500 2WD Cargo	A-4	4.3/6	16
GMC			
Savana 1500 2WD (cargo)	A-4	4.3/6	16
VANS, PASSENGER			
CHEVROLET			
Express 1500 2WD Passenger	A-4	5.3/8	14‡
Express 1500 AWD Passenger	A-4	5.3/8	14‡
FORD			
E150 Wagon FFV	A-4	4.6/8	14‡
GMC			
Savana 1500 2WD (Passenger)	A-4	5.3/8	14‡
Savana 1500 AWD (Passenger)	A-4	5.3/8	14‡
SPECIAL PURPOSE VEHICLES			
FORD			
Transit Connect Van 2WD	A-S6	1.6/4	25
Transit Connect Wagon FWD	A-S6	1.6/4	25
MINIVANS			
MAZDA			
5	A-S5	2.5/4	24
5	M-6	2.5/4	24
SMALL SPORT UTILITY VEHICLES			
TOYOTA			
RAV4 EV	AV		76*
SUBARU			
XV Crosstrek Hybrid AWD	AV	2.0/4	31
STANDARD SPORT UTILITY VEHICLES			
TOYOTA			
Highlander Hybrid 4WD	AV-S6	3.5/6	28
Highlander Hybrid 4WD LE Plus	AV-S6	3.5/6	28

* This is an electric vehicle. Since electricity is not measured in gallons, a conversion factor is used to translate the fuel economy into miles per gallon of gasoline equivalent (MPGe).

† This vehicle is a plug-in hybrid, which runs on both gasoline and electricity. Since electricity is not measured in gallons, a conversion factor is used to translate the fuel economy when running on electricity into miles per gallon of gasoline equivalent (MPGe). The Combined MPGe estimate includes both city and highway driving and gasoline and electric energy use.

‡ When operated on gasoline

2014 MODEL YEAR VEHICLES

This section contains the fuel economy values for 2014 model year vehicles. Additional information for alternative fuel vehicles can be found on pages 32–34 and 37–41. Alternative fuel vehicles are highlighted with a light blue background, and those that can use two kinds of fuel, such as flexible fuel vehicles, have an entry for each fuel type. The most fuel-efficient vehicles per class are listed in blue boldface type and marked with a red pointer (▶).

Manufacturer Model Configuration (trans, eng size, cyl)	MPG		Annual Fuel Cost	GHG Rating	Notes
	Comb	City/Hwy			

TWO SEATERS

ASTON MARTIN
V8 Vantage
AM-7, 4.7L, 8cyl	16	14/21	$3,550	3	P Tax
M-6, 4.7L, 8cyl	15	13/19	$3,800	2	P Tax

V8 Vantage S
AM-7, 4.7L, 8cyl	16	14/21	$3,550	3	P Tax
M-6, 4.7L, 8cyl	15	13/19	$3,800	2	P Tax

AUDI
R8
AM-S7, 4.2L, 8cyl	17	14/23	$3,350	3	P Tax
M-6, 4.2L, 8cyl	14	11/20	$4,050	2	P Tax
AM-S7, 5.2L, 10cyl	16	13/22	$3,550	3	P Tax
M-6, 5.2L, 10cyl	14	12/19	$4,050	2	P Tax

R8 Spyder
AM-S7, 4.2L, 8cyl	17	14/23	$3,350	3	P Tax
M-6, 4.2L, 8cyl	14	11/20	$4,050	2	P Tax
AM-S7, 5.2L, 10cyl	16	13/22	$3,550	3	P Tax
M-6, 5.2L, 10cyl	14	12/19	$4,050	2	P Tax

TT Roadster quattro
AM-S6, 2.0L, 4cyl	26	22/31	$2,200	7	P T

BMW
Z4 sDrive28i
A-S8, 2.0L, 4cyl	26	22/33	$2,200	7	P T
M-6, 2.0L, 4cyl	26	22/34	$2,200	7	P T SS

Z4 sDrive35i
AM-S7, 3.0L, 6cyl	20	17/24	$2,850	5	P T
M-6, 3.0L, 6cyl	21	19/26	$2,700	5	P T

Z4 sDrive35is
AM-S7, 3.0L, 6cyl	20	17/24	$2,850	5	P T

BUGATTI
Veyron
AM-S7, 8.0L, 16cyl	10	8/15	$5,650	1	P T Tax

CHEVROLET
Corvette
A-S6, 6.2L, 8cyl	20	16/28	$2,850	5	P
M-7, 6.2L, 8cyl	21	17/29	$2,700	5	P

FERRARI
458 Italia
AM-7, 4.5L, 8cyl	14	13/17	$4,050	2	P Tax
AM-7, 4.5L, 8cyl	15	13/17	$3,800	2	P Tax SS

458 Spider
AM-7, 4.5L, 8cyl	15	13/17	$3,800	2	P Tax SS
AM-7, 4.5L, 8cyl	14	13/17	$4,050	2	P Tax

F12
AM-7, 6.3L, 12cyl	13	12/16	$4,350	1	P Tax SS
AM-7, 6.3L, 12cyl	13	11/16	$4,350	1	P Tax

HONDA
CR-Z
▶ AV-S7, 1.5L, 4cyl	37	36/39	$1,400	9	HEV SS
M-6, 1.5L, 4cyl	34	31/38	$1,500	8	HEV SS

JAGUAR
F-Type Convertible
A-S8, 3.0L, 6cyl	23	20/28	$2,450	6	P S SS

F-Type S Convertible
A-S8, 3.0L, 6cyl	22	19/27	$2,600	5	P S SS

F-Type V8 S Convertible
A-S8, 5.0L, 8cyl	18	16/23	$3,150	4	P S SS

LAMBORGHINI
Aventador Coupe
AM-S7, 6.5L, 12cyl	13	11/18	$4,350	1	P Tax SS

Aventador Roadster
AM-S7, 6.5L, 12cyl	12	10/16	$4,700	1	P Tax SS

Aventador Veneno Coupe
AM-S7, 6.5L, 12cyl	13	11/17	$4,350	1	P Tax

ABBREVIATIONS:

▶	Highest MPG in Class
2WD	Two-Wheel Drive
4WD	Four-Wheel Drive
A	Automatic Transmission
A-S	Automatic Transmission-Select Shift
AM	Automated Manual
AM-S	Automated Manual-Selectable
AV	Continuously Variable Transmission
AV-S	Continuously Variable Transmision with Select Shift
AWD	All-Wheel Drive
City	MPG on City Test Procedure
Cyl	Cylinders
Comb	Combined
D	Ultra-Low Sulfur Diesel

E85	85% Ethanol/15% Gasoline
Eng Size	Engine Volume in Liters
EV	ELectric Vehicle
FFV	Flexible Fuel Vehicle
FWD	Front-Wheel Drive
Gas	Regular Gasoline
GHG	Greenhouse Gas
HEV	Hybrid-Electric Vehicle
Hwy	MPG on Highway Test Procedure
i-ELOOP	Mazda Optional Technology Package
Li-Ion	Lithium Ion
LWB	Long Wheel Base
M	Manual Transmission
Mid	Midgrade Gasoline
Mode	Multimode Transmission

MPG	Miles per Gallon
NA	Not Available
Ni-MH	Nickel-Metal Hydride
ORP	Off-Road Package
P	Premium Gasoline Recommended
PHEV	Plug-in Hybrid Electric Vehicle
PR	Premium Gasoline Required
PT4WD	Part-time 4WD
PZEV	Partial Zero-Emission Vehicles
S	Supercharger
SIDI	Spark Ignition Direct Injection
SS	Stop-Start Technology
T	Turbocharger
Tax	Subject to Gas Guzzler Tax
Trans	Transmission

Manufacturer Model Configuration (trans, eng size, cyl)	MPG Comb	MPG City/Hwy	Annual Fuel Cost	GHG Rating	Notes
Gallardo Coupe					
AM-S6, 5.2L, 10cyl	16	13/20	$3,550	3	P Tax
M-6, 5.2L, 10cyl	15	12/20	$3,800	2	P Tax
Gallardo Spyder					
AM-S6, 5.2L, 10cyl	16	13/20	$3,550	3	P Tax
M-6, 5.2L, 10cyl	14	12/20	$4,050	2	P Tax
MAZDA					
MX-5					
A-S6, 2.0L, 4cyl	23	21/28	$2,450	6	P
M-5, 2.0L, 4cyl	25	22/28	$2,250	6	P
M-6, 2.0L, 4cyl	24	21/28	$2,350	6	P
MERCEDES-BENZ					
SL550					
A-7, 4.7L, 8cyl	20	18/25	$2,850	5	P T SS
SL63 AMG					
A-7, 5.5L, 8cyl	19	16/25	$3,000	4	P T SS
SL65 AMG					
A-7, 6.0L, 12cyl	17	14/21	$3,350	3	P T Tax SS
SLK250					
A-7, 1.8L, 4cyl	26	23/33	$2,200	7	P T
M-6, 1.8L, 4cyl	26	22/32	$2,200	7	P T
SLK350					
A-7, 3.5L, 6cyl	24	21/29	$2,350	6	P SS
SLK55 AMG					
A-7, 5.5L, 8cyl	22	19/28	$2,600	5	P SS
SLS AMG Black Series Coupe					
AM-7, 6.2L, 8cyl	14	13/17	$4,050	2	P Tax
SLS AMG Coupe					
AM-7, 6.2L, 8cyl	15	13/19	$3,800	2	P Tax
SLS AMG GT Coupe					
AM-7, 6.2L, 8cyl	15	13/19	$3,800	2	P Tax
SLS AMG GT Roadster					
AM-7, 6.2L, 8cyl	15	13/19	$3,800	2	P Tax
SLS AMG Roadster					
AM-7, 6.2L, 8cyl	15	13/19	$3,800	2	P Tax
MINI					
Cooper Clubvan					
A-S6, 1.6L, 4cyl	30	27/35	$1,900	8	P
M-6, 1.6L, 4cyl	31	28/35	$1,850	8	P
Cooper Coupe					
A-S6, 1.6L, 4cyl	31	28/36	$1,850	8	P
M-6, 1.6L, 4cyl	32	29/37	$1,800	8	P
Cooper Roadster					
A-S6, 1.6L, 4cyl	30	27/35	$1,900	8	P
M-6, 1.6L, 4cyl	31	28/35	$1,850	8	P
Cooper S Coupe					
A-S6, 1.6L, 4cyl	30	26/35	$1,900	8	P T
M-6, 1.6L, 4cyl	30	26/35	$1,900	8	P T
Cooper S Roadster					
A-S6, 1.6L, 4cyl	30	26/35	$1,900	8	P T
M-6, 1.6L, 4cyl	30	26/35	$1,900	8	P T
John Cooper Works Coupe					
A-S6, 1.6L, 4cyl	30	26/35	$1,900	8	P T
M-6, 1.6L, 4cyl	30	26/35	$1,900	8	P T
John Cooper Works Roadster					
A-S6, 1.6L, 4cyl	30	26/35	$1,900	8	P T
M-6, 1.6L, 4cyl	30	26/35	$1,900	8	P T
NISSAN					
370Z					
A-S7, 3.7L, 6cyl	22	19/26	$2,600	5	P
M-6, 3.7L, 6cyl	21	18/26	$2,700	5	P
370Z Roadster					
A-S7, 3.7L, 6cyl	21	18/25	$2,700	5	P
M-6, 3.7L, 6cyl	20	17/25	$2,850	5	P
PORSCHE					
911 GT3					
AM-S7, 3.8L, 6cyl	17	15/20	$3,350	3	P Tax
Boxster					
AM-S7, 2.7L, 6cyl	26	22/32	$2,200	7	P
M-6, 2.7L, 6cyl	24	20/30	$2,350	6	P
Boxster S					
AM-S7, 3.4L, 6cyl	24	21/30	$2,350	6	P
M-6, 3.4L, 6cyl	23	20/28	$2,450	6	P
Cayman					
AM-S7, 2.7L, 6cyl	26	22/32	$2,200	7	P
M-6, 2.7L, 6cyl	24	20/30	$2,350	6	P
Cayman S					
AM-S7, 3.4L, 6cyl	24	21/30	$2,350	6	P
M-6, 3.4L, 6cyl	23	20/28	$2,450	6	P
SMART					
fortwo cabriolet					
AM5, 1.0L, 3cyl	36	34/38	$1,600	9	P
fortwo coupe					
AM5, 1.0L, 3cyl	36	34/38	$1,600	9	P
fortwo electric drive convertible					
▶ A-1	107	122/93	$600	10	EV
fortwo electric drive coupe					
▶ A-1	107	122/93	$600	10	EV
SRT					
Viper					
M-6, 8.4L, 10cyl	15	12/19	$3,800	2	P Tax

MINICOMPACT CARS

Manufacturer Model Configuration (trans, eng size, cyl)	MPG Comb	MPG City/Hwy	Annual Fuel Cost	GHG Rating	Notes
ASTON MARTIN					
DB9					
A-S6, 5.9L, 12cyl	15	13/19	$3,800	2	P Tax
Vanquish					
A-S6, 5.9L, 12cyl	15	13/19	$3,800	2	P Tax
FERRARI					
California					
AM-7, 4.3L, 8cyl	16	14/19	$3,550	3	P Tax SS
AM-7, 4.3L, 8cyl	15	13/19	$3,800	2	P Tax
FIAT					
500					
A-6, 1.4L, 4cyl	30	27/34	$1,900	8	P
M-5, 1.4L, 4cyl	34	31/40	$1,650	8	P
M-5, 1.4L, 4cyl	30	28/34	$1,900	8	P T

Manufacturer Model Configuration (trans, eng size, cyl)	MPG Comb	MPG City/Hwy	Annual Fuel Cost	GHG Rating	Notes
500 Abarth					
M-5, 1.4L, 4cyl	30	28/34	$1,900	8	P T
500e					
▶ A-1	116	122/108	$500	10	EV
JAGUAR					
XK					
A-S6, 5.0L, 8cyl	19	16/24	$3,000	4	P
A-S6, 5.0L, 8cyl	18	15/22	$3,150	4	P S
XK Convertible					
A-S6, 5.0L, 8cyl	18	16/22	$3,150	4	P
A-S6, 5.0L, 8cyl	17	15/22	$3,350	3	P S
LOTUS					
Evora					
A-S6, 3.5L, 6cyl	22	19/28	$2,600	5	P
A-S6, 3.5L, 6cyl	22	19/28	$2,600	5	P S
M-6, 3.5L, 6cyl	21	18/26	$2,700	5	P
M-6, 3.5L, 6cyl	20	17/26	$2,850	5	P S
MINI					
Cooper Convertible					
A-S6, 1.6L, 4cyl	30	27/35	$1,900	8	P
M-6, 1.6L, 4cyl	31	28/35	$1,850	8	P
Cooper S Convertible					
A-S6, 1.6L, 4cyl	30	26/35	$1,900	8	P T
M-6, 1.6L, 4cyl	30	26/35	$1,900	8	P T
John Cooper Works Convertible					
A-S6, 1.6L, 4cyl	30	26/35	$1,900	8	P T
M-6, 1.6L, 4cyl	30	26/35	$1,900	8	P T
PORSCHE					
911 Carrera					
AM-S7, 3.4L, 6cyl	23	20/28	$2,450	6	P
M-7, 3.4L, 6cyl	22	19/27	$2,600	5	P
911 Carrera 4					
AM-S7, 3.4L, 6cyl	23	20/28	$2,450	6	P
M-7, 3.4L, 6cyl	22	19/27	$2,600	5	P
911 Carrera 4 Cabriolet					
AM-S7, 3.4L, 6cyl	22	20/27	$2,600	5	P
M-7, 3.4L, 6cyl	21	19/26	$2,700	5	P
911 Carrera 4S					
AM-S7, 3.8L, 6cyl	22	19/26	$2,600	5	P
M-7, 3.8L, 6cyl	21	18/26	$2,700	5	P
911 Carrera 4S Cabriolet					
AM-S7, 3.8L, 6cyl	21	19/26	$2,700	5	P
M-7, 3.8L, 6cyl	21	18/26	$2,700	5	P
911 Carrera Cabriolet					
AM-S7, 3.4L, 6cyl	23	20/28	$2,450	6	P
M-7, 3.4L, 6cyl	22	19/27	$2,600	5	P
911 Carrera S					
AM-S7, 3.8L, 6cyl	22	19/27	$2,600	5	P
M-7, 3.8L, 6cyl	22	19/27	$2,600	5	P
911 Carrera S Cabriolet					
AM-S7, 3.8L, 6cyl	22	19/27	$2,600	5	P
M-7, 3.8L, 6cyl	22	19/27	$2,600	5	P
911 Targa 4					
AM-S7, 3.4L, 6cyl	22	19/26	$2,600	5	P
M-7, 3.4L, 6cyl	21	18/26	$2,700	5	P
911 Targa 4S					
AM-S7, 3.8L, 6cyl	21	18/25	$2,700	5	P
M-7, 3.8L, 6cyl	21	18/26	$2,700	5	P
911 Turbo					
AM-S7, 3.8L, 6cyl	20	17/24	$2,850	5	P T
911 Turbo Cabriolet					
AM-S7, 3.8L, 6cyl	20	17/24	$2,850	5	P T
911 Turbo S					
AM-S7, 3.8L, 6cyl	20	17/24	$2,850	5	P T
911 Turbo S Cabriolet					
AM-S7, 3.8L, 6cyl	20	17/24	$2,850	5	P T
SCION					
FR-S					
A-S6, 2.0L, 4cyl	28	25/34	$2,000	7	P
M-6, 2.0L, 4cyl	25	22/30	$2,250	6	P
iQ					
▶ AV, 1.3L, 4cyl	37	36/37	$1,400	9	
SUBARU					
BRZ					
A-S6, 2.0L, 4cyl	28	25/34	$2,000	7	P
M-6, 2.0L, 4cyl	25	22/30	$2,250	6	P

SUBCOMPACT CARS

Manufacturer Model Configuration (trans, eng size, cyl)	MPG Comb	MPG City/Hwy	Annual Fuel Cost	GHG Rating	Notes
ASTON MARTIN					
Rapide S					
A-S6, 5.9L, 12cyl	15	13/19	$3,800	2	P Tax
AUDI					
A5 Cabriolet					
AV-S8, 2.0L, 4cyl	27	24/32	$2,100	7	P T
A5 Cabriolet quattro					
A-S8, 2.0L, 4cyl	24	20/29	$2,350	6	Gas P T
	16	14/20	$2,850	6	E85
A5 quattro					
M-6, 2.0L, 4cyl	26	22/32	$2,200	7	P T
A-S8, 2.0L, 4cyl	24	20/29	$2,350	6	Gas P T
	16	14/20	$2,850	6	E85
RS 5					
AM-S7, 4.2L, 8cyl	18	16/23	$3,150	4	P
RS 5 Cabriolet					
AM-S7, 4.2L, 8cyl	18	16/22	$3,150	4	P
S5					
AM-S7, 3.0L, 6cyl	21	18/28	$2,700	5	P S
M-6, 3.0L, 6cyl	20	17/26	$2,850	5	P S
S5 Cabriolet					
AM-S7, 3.0L, 6cyl	21	18/26	$2,700	5	P S
TT Coupe quattro					
AM-S6, 2.0L, 4cyl	26	22/31	$2,200	7	P T
BENTLEY					
Continental GT Speed Convertible					
A-S8, 6.0L, 12cyl	15	12/20	$3,800	2	Gas P T Tax
	11	9/15	$4,150	2	E85

Manufacturer Model Configuration (trans, eng size, cyl)	MPG Comb	MPG City/Hwy	Annual Fuel Cost	GHG Rating	Notes
Continental GTC					
A-S8, 4.0L, 8cyl	17	14/24	$3,350	3	P T Tax
A-S8, 6.0L, 12cyl	15	12/20	$3,800	2	Gas P T Tax
	11	9/15	$4,150	2	E85
BMW					
228i					
A-S8, 2.0L, 4cyl	28	23/36	$2,000	7	P T SS
M-6, 2.0L, 4cyl	26	22/34	$2,200	7	P T SS
428i Convertible					
A-S8, 2.0L, 4cyl	27	23/34	$2,100	7	P T SS
640i Convertible					
A-S8, 3.0L, 6cyl	24	20/30	$2,350	6	P T SS
640i Coupe					
A-S8, 3.0L, 6cyl	25	22/32	$2,250	6	P T SS
640i xDrive Convertible					
A-S8, 3.0L, 6cyl	23	20/29	$2,450	6	P T SS
640i xDrive Coupe					
A-S8, 3.0L, 6cyl	23	20/29	$2,450	6	P T SS
650i Convertible					
A-S8, 4.4L, 8cyl	20	17/25	$2,850	5	P T SS
650i Coupe					
A-S8, 4.4L, 8cyl	20	17/25	$2,850	5	P T SS
650i xDrive Convertible					
A-S8, 4.4L, 8cyl	19	16/24	$3,000	4	P T SS
650i xDrive Coupe					
A-S8, 4.4L, 8cyl	19	16/24	$3,000	4	P T
M235i					
A-S8, 3.0L, 6cyl	25	22/32	$2,250	6	P T SS
M-6, 3.0L, 6cyl	23	19/28	$2,450	6	P T SS
M6 Convertible					
AM-S7, 4.4L, 8cyl	16	14/20	$3,550	3	P T Tax SS
M-6, 4.4L, 8cyl	17	15/22	$3,350	3	P T Tax SS
M6 Coupe					
AM-S7, 4.4L, 8cyl	16	14/20	$3,550	3	P T Tax SS
M-6, 4.4L, 8cyl	17	15/22	$3,350	3	P T Tax SS
CADILLAC					
ELR					
AV, 1.4L, 4cyl		See page 34			PHEV SS
CHEVROLET					
Spark					
AV, 1.2L, 4cyl	34	30/39	$1,500	8	
M-5, 1.2L, 4cyl	34	31/39	$1,500	8	
Spark EV					
▶ A-1	119	128/109	$500	10	EV
FORD					
Fiesta FWD					
AM-6, 1.6L, 4cyl	32	29/39	$1,600	8	
M-5, 1.6L, 4cyl	31	27/38	$1,650	8	
Fiesta SFE FWD					
▶ M-5, 1.0L, 3cyl	37	32/45	$1,400	9	T
AM-6, 1.6L, 4cyl	34	30/41	$1,500	8	

Manufacturer Model Configuration (trans, eng size, cyl)	MPG Comb	MPG City/Hwy	Annual Fuel Cost	GHG Rating	Notes
Mustang					
A-6, 3.7L, 6cyl	23	19/31	$2,250	6	
M-6, 3.7L, 6cyl	22	19/29	$2,350	5	
A-6, 5.0L, 6cyl	20	18/25	$2,600	5	
M-6, 5.0L, 8cyl	19	15/26	$2,700	4	
M-6, 5.8L, 8cyl	18	15/24	$3,150	4	P S
Mustang Convertible					
A-6, 3.7L, 6cyl	23	19/30	$2,250	6	
HYUNDAI					
Genesis Coupe					
A-8, 2.0L, 4cyl	21	17/27	$2,700	5	P T
M-6, 2.0L, 4cyl	22	19/27	$2,600	5	P T
A-8, 3.8L, 6cyl	19	16/25	$3,000	4	P
M-6, 3.8L, 6cyl	19	16/24	$3,000	4	P
INFINITI					
Q60 AWD Coupe					
A-S7, 3.7L, 6cyl	20	18/25	$2,850	5	P
Q60 Convertible					
A-S7, 3.7L, 6cyl	20	18/26	$2,850	5	P
M-6, 3.7L, 6cyl	19	16/24	$3,000	4	P
Q60 Coupe					
A-S7, 3.7L, 6cyl	22	19/27	$2,600	5	P
M-6, 3.7L, 6cyl	20	17/25	$2,850	5	P
LEXUS					
IS 250 C					
A-S6, 2.5L, 6cyl	24	21/30	$2,350	6	P
IS 350 C					
A-S6, 3.5L, 6cyl	22	19/27	$2,600	5	P
IS F					
A-S8, 5.0L, 8cyl	18	16/23	$3,150	4	P
MASERATI					
GranTurismo					
A-6, 4.7L, 8cyl	16	13/21	$3,550	3	P Tax
GranTurismo Convertible					
A-6, 4.7L, 8cyl	15	13/20	$3,800	2	P Tax
MERCEDES-BENZ					
C250 Coupe					
A-7, 1.8L, 4cyl	25	22/31	$2,250	6	P T
C350 4matic Coupe					
A-7, 3.5L, 6cyl	22	19/27	$2,600	5	P SS
C350 Coupe					
A-7, 3.5L, 6cyl	23	20/28	$2,450	6	P SS
C63 AMG Coupe					
A-7, 6.2L, 8cyl	15	13/19	$3,800	2	P Tax
E350 4matic Coupe					
A-7, 3.5L, 6cyl	23	20/28	$2,450	6	P SS
A-7, 3.5L, 6cyl	23	20/28	$2,450	6	P PZEV SS
A-7, 3.5L, 6cyl	23	20/28	$2,450	6	Gas P SS
	17	15/21	$2,700	6	E85
E350 Convertible					
A-7, 3.5L, 6cyl	22	19/28	$2,600	5	P SS
A-7, 3.5L, 6cyl	23	20/28	$2,450	6	Gas P SS
	17	14/21	$2,700	6	E85

Manufacturer Model Configuration (trans, eng size, cyl)	MPG Comb	City/Hwy	Annual Fuel Cost	GHG Rating	Notes
E350 Coupe					
A-7, 3.5L, 6cyl	24	20/30	$2,350	6	P PZEV SS
A-7, 3.5L, 6cyl	23	20/28	$2,450	6	P SS
A-7, 3.5L, 6cyl	23	20/29	$2,450	6	Gas P SS
	18	15/22	$2,550	6	E85
E550 Convertible					
A-7, 4.7L, 8cyl	20	17/26	$2,850	5	P T SS
E550 Coupe					
A-7, 4.7L, 8cyl	21	18/26	$2,700	5	P T SS
MINI					
Cooper Clubman					
A-S6, 1.6L, 4cyl	30	27/35	$1,900	8	P
M-6, 1.6L, 4cyl	31	28/35	$1,850	8	P
Cooper S Clubman					
A-S6, 1.6L, 4cyl	30	26/35	$1,900	8	P T
M-6, 1.6L, 4cyl	30	26/35	$1,900	8	P T
John Cooper Works Clubman					
A-S6, 1.6L, 4cyl	30	26/35	$1,900	8	P T
M-6, 1.6L, 4cyl	30	26/35	$1,900	8	P T
NISSAN					
GT-R					
AM-6, 3.8L, 6cyl	19	16/23	$3,000	4	P T
ROUSH PERFORMANCE					
Stage 3 Mustang					
A-6, 5.0L, 8cyl	18	15/22	$3,150	4	P S
M-6, 5.0L, 8cyl	17	14/22	$3,350	3	P S Tax
SCION					
xD					
A-4, 1.8L, 4cyl	29	27/33	$1,800	7	
M-5, 1.8L, 4cyl	29	27/33	$1,800	7	
VOLKSWAGEN					
Beetle Convertible					
A-S6, 1.8L, 4cyl	27	24/32	$1,900	7	T
AM-S6, 2.0L, 4cyl	25	23/29	$2,250	6	P T
M-6, 2.0L, 4cyl	26	23/31	$2,200	7	P T
A-S6, 2.5L, 5cyl	23	21/27	$2,250	6	
AM-S6, 2.0L, 4cyl	31	28/37	$1,950	7	D T
M-6, 2.0L, 4cyl	32	28/41	$1,900	7	D T
Eos					
AM-S6, 2.0L, 4cyl	25	22/30	$2,250	6	P T

COMPACT CARS

Manufacturer Model Configuration (trans, eng size, cyl)	MPG Comb	City/Hwy	Annual Fuel Cost	GHG Rating	Notes
ACURA					
ILX					
A-S5, 2.0L, 4cyl	28	24/35	$2,000	7	P
M-6, 2.4L, 4cyl	25	22/31	$2,250	6	P
ILX Hybrid					
AV-S7, 1.5L, 4cyl	38	39/38	$1,500	9	P HEV SS
TSX					
A-S5, 2.4L, 4cyl	26	22/31	$2,200	7	P
M-6, 2.4L, 4cyl	24	21/29	$2,350	6	P
A-S5, 3.5L, 6cyl	23	19/28	$2,450	6	P

Manufacturer Model Configuration (trans, eng size, cyl)	MPG Comb	City/Hwy	Annual Fuel Cost	GHG Rating	Notes
AUDI					
A4					
AV-S8, 2.0L, 4cyl	27	24/32	$2,100	7	P T
A4 quattro					
M-6, 2.0L, 4cyl	26	22/32	$2,200	7	P T
A-S8, 2.0L, 4cyl	24	20/29	$2,350	6	Gas P T
	16	14/20	$2,850	6	E85
S4					
AM-S7, 3.0L, 6cyl	21	18/28	$2,700	5	P S
M-6, 3.0L, 6cyl	20	17/26	$2,850	5	P S
BENTLEY					
Continental GT					
A-S8, 4.0L, 8cyl	18	15/24	$3,150	4	P T
A-S8, 6.0L, 12cyl	15	12/21	$3,800	2	Gas P T Tax
	11	9/15	$4,150	2	E85
BMW					
320i					
A-S8, 2.0L, 4cyl	28	24/36	$2,000	7	P T SS
M-6, 2.0L, 4cyl	27	23/36	$2,100	7	P T SS
320i xDrive					
A-S8, 2.0L, 4cyl	27	23/35	$2,100	7	P T SS
328d					
A-S8, 2.0L, 4cyl	37	32/45	$1,650	8	D T
328d xDrive					
A-S8, 2.0L, 4cyl	35	31/43	$1,750	8	D T
328i					
A-S8, 2.0L, 4cyl	27	23/35	$2,100	7	P T SS
M-6, 2.0L, 4cyl	26	22/34	$2,200	7	P T SS
328i xDrive					
A-S8, 2.0L, 4cyl	26	22/33	$2,200	7	P T SS
335i					
A-S8, 3.0L, 6cyl	25	22/32	$2,250	6	P T SS
M-6, 3.0L, 6cyl	23	20/30	$2,450	6	P T SS
335i xDrive					
A-S8, 3.0L, 6cyl	24	20/30	$2,350	6	P T SS
M-6, 3.0L, 6cyl	23	20/28	$2,450	6	P T SS
428i Coupe					
A-S8, 2.0L, 4cyl	27	23/35	$2,100	7	P T SS
M-6, 2.0L, 4cyl	26	22/34	$2,200	7	P T SS
428i xDrive Coupe					
A-S8, 2.0L, 4cyl	26	22/33	$2,200	7	P T SS
435i Coupe					
A-S8, 3.0L, 6cyl	25	22/32	$2,250	6	P T SS
M-6, 3.0L, 6cyl	23	20/30	$2,450	6	P T SS
435i xDrive Coupe					
A-S8, 3.0L, 6cyl	24	20/30	$2,350	6	P T SS
M-6, 3.0L, 6cyl	23	20/28	$2,450	6	P T SS
640i Gran Coupe					
A-S8, 3.0L, 6cyl	24	20/30	$2,350	6	P T SS
640i xDrive Gran Coupe					
A-S8, 3.0L, 6cyl	23	20/29	$2,450	6	P T SS
650i Gran Coupe					
A-S8, 4.4L, 8cyl	20	17/25	$2,850	5	P T SS

Manufacturer Model Configuration (trans, eng size, cyl)	MPG Comb	MPG City/Hwy	Annual Fuel Cost	GHG Rating	Notes
650i xDrive Gran Coupe					
A-S8, 4.4L, 8cyl	19	16/24	$3,000	4	P T SS
ActiveHybrid 3					
A-S8, 3.0L, 6cyl	28	25/33	$2,000	7	P T HEV SS
M6 Gran Coupe					
AM-S7, 4.4L, 8cyl	16	14/20	$3,550	3	P T Tax SS
M-6, 4.4L, 8cyl	17	15/22	$3,350	3	P T Tax SS
BUICK					
Verano					
A-S6, 2.0L, 4cyl	24	21/30	$2,150	6	T
M-6, 2.0L, 4cyl	24	20/31	$2,150	6	T
A-S6, 2.4L, 4cyl	25	21/32	$2,050	6	
CADILLAC					
ATS					
A-S6, 2.0L, 4cyl	24	21/31	$2,150	6	T
M-6, 2.0L, 4cyl	23	19/30	$2,250	6	T
A-S6, 2.5L, 4cyl	26	22/33	$2,000	7	
A-S6, 3.6L, 6cyl	22	18/28	$2,350	5	
ATS AWD					
A-S6, 2.0L, 4cyl	23	20/29	$2,250	6	T
A-S6, 3.6L, 6cyl	21	18/26	$2,450	5	
CHEVROLET					
Camaro					
A-S6, 3.6L, 6cyl	21	18/27	$2,450	5	
A-6, 3.6L, 6cyl	22	19/30	$2,350	5	
M-6, 3.6L, 6cyl	20	17/28	$2,600	5	
A-S6, 6.2L, 8cyl	18	15/24	$2,850	4	
A-S6, 6.2L, 8cyl	14	12/18	$4,050	2	P S Tax
M-6, 6.2L, 8cyl	19	16/24	$2,700	4	
M-6, 6.2L, 8cyl	16	14/19	$3,550	3	P S Tax
Sonic					
A-S6, 1.4L, 4cyl	31	27/37	$1,650	8	T
M-6, 1.4L, 4cyl	33	29/40	$1,550	8	T
A-S6, 1.8L, 4cyl	28	25/35	$1,850	7	
M-5, 1.8L, 4cyl	30	26/35	$1,700	8	
Sonic RS					
A-S6, 1.4L, 4cyl	28	25/33	$1,850	7	T
M-6, 1.4L, 4cyl	30	27/34	$1,700	8	T
Volt					
AV, 1.4L, 4cyl		See page 34			PHEV SS
CHRYSLER					
200 Convertible					
A-6, 2.4L, 4cyl	22	18/29	$2,350	5	
A-6, 3.6L, 6cyl	22	19/29	$2,350	5	Gas
	16	14/21	$2,850	6	E85
FORD					
Fiesta ST FWD					
M-6, 1.6L, 4cyl	29	26/35	$1,800	7	T
Focus Electric					
▶ A-1	105	110/99	$600	10	EV
Focus FWD					
AM-6, 2.0L, 4cyl	31	27/37	$1,650	8	
A-S6, 2.0L, 4cyl	31	27/37	$1,650	8	
M-5, 2.0L, 4cyl	30	26/36	$1,700	8	
M-6, 2.0L, 4cyl	26	23/32	$2,000	7	T

Manufacturer Model Configuration (trans, eng size, cyl)	MPG Comb	MPG City/Hwy	Annual Fuel Cost	GHG Rating	Notes
Focus FWD FFV					
AM-6, 2.0L, 4cyl	30	26/37	$1,700	8	Gas
	23	20/28	$2,000	8	E85
A-S6, 2.0L, 4cyl	30	26/37	$1,700	8	Gas
	23	20/28	$2,000	8	E85
M-5, 2.0L, 4cyl	30	26/36	$1,700	8	Gas
	22	19/26	$2,100	8	E85
Focus SFE FWD FFV					
AM-6, 2.0L, 4cyl	33	28/40	$1,550	8	Gas
	23	20/28	$2,000	8	E85
HONDA					
Civic Hybrid					
AV, 1.5L, 4cyl	45	44/47	$1,150	10	HEV SS
Civic Natural Gas					
A-5, 1.8L, 4cyl	31	27/38	$1,000	9	CNG
Insight					
AV-S7, 1.3L, 4cyl	42	41/44	$1,250	9	HEV SS
AV, 1.3L, 4cyl	42	41/44	$1,250	9	HEV SS
HYUNDAI					
Accent					
A-6, 1.6L, 4cyl	31	27/37	$1,650	8	
M-6, 1.6L, 4cyl	31	27/38	$1,650	8	
Veloster					
AM-6, 1.6L, 4cyl	31	28/36	$1,650	8	
A-6, 1.6L, 4cyl	27	24/31	$1,900	7	T
M-6, 1.6L, 4cyl	30	26/35	$1,700	8	
M-6, 1.6L, 4cyl	28	24/33	$1,850	7	T
INFINITI					
Q50 Hybrid					
A-S7, 3.5L, 6cyl	31	29/36	$1,850	8	P HEV SS
Q50 Hybrid AWD					
A-S7, 3.5L, 6cyl	30	28/35	$1,900	8	P HEV SS
Q50S Hybrid					
A-S7, 3.5L, 6cyl	30	28/34	$1,900	8	P HEV SS
Q50S Hybrid AWD					
A-S7, 3.5L, 6cyl	28	27/31	$2,000	7	P HEV SS
KIA					
Forte Koup					
A-6, 1.6L, 4cyl	25	22/30	$2,050	6	T
M-6, 1.6L, 4cyl	25	22/29	$2,050	6	T
A-6, 2.0L, 4cyl	28	25/34	$1,850	7	
M-6, 2.0L, 4cyl	27	24/33	$1,900	7	
Rio					
A-6, 1.6L, 4cyl	31	27/37	$1,650	8	
M-6, 1.6L, 4cyl	31	27/37	$1,650	8	
Rio Eco					
A-6, 1.6L, 4cyl	31	28/37	$1,650	8	SS

Manufacturer Model Configuration (trans, eng size, cyl)	MPG Comb	MPG City/Hwy	Annual Fuel Cost	GHG Rating	Notes
LEXUS					
CT 200h					
AV, 1.8L, 4cyl	42	43/40	$1,250	9	HEV SS
IS 250					
A-S6, 2.5L, 6cyl	24	21/30	$2,350	6	P
IS 250 AWD					
A-S6, 2.5L, 6cyl	23	20/27	$2,450	6	P
IS 350					
A-S8, 3.5L, 6cyl	22	19/28	$2,600	5	P
IS 350 AWD					
A-S6, 3.5L, 6cyl	21	19/26	$2,700	5	P
MAZDA					
2					
A-4, 1.5L, 4cyl	30	28/34	$1,700	8	
M-5, 1.5L, 4cyl	32	29/35	$1,600	8	
3 4-Door					
A-S6, 2.0L, 4cyl	34	30/41	$1,500	8	
M-6, 2.0L, 4cyl	33	29/41	$1,550	8	
A-S6, 2.5L, 4cyl	32	28/39	$1,600	8	i-ELOOP
A-S6, 2.5L, 4cyl	32	28/39	$1,600	8	
MERCEDES-BENZ					
C250					
A-7, 1.8L, 4cyl	25	22/31	$2,250	6	P T
C300 4matic					
A-7, 3.5L, 6cyl	23	20/29	$2,450	6	P PZEV SS
A-7, 3.5L, 6cyl	22	20/27	$2,600	5	P SS
A-7, 3.5L, 6cyl	22	20/27	$2,600	5	Gas P SS
	16	14/20	$2,850	6	E85
C350					
A-7, 3.5L, 6cyl	24	20/29	$2,350	6	P PZEV SS
A-7, 3.5L, 6cyl	23	20/29	$2,450	6	P SS
A-7, 3.5L, 6cyl	23	20/29	$2,450	6	Gas P SS
	17	15/21	$2,700	6	E85
C63 AMG					
A-7, 6.2L, 8cyl	15	13/19	$3,800	2	P Tax
CL550 4matic					
A-7, 4.7L, 8cyl	18	15/24	$3,150	4	P T
CL600					
A-5, 5.5L, 12cyl	14	12/18	$4,050	2	P T Tax
CL63 AMG					
A-7, 5.5L, 8cyl	18	15/22	$3,150	4	P T SS
CL65 AMG					
A-5, 6.0L, 12cyl	14	12/18	$4,050	2	P T Tax
CLA250					
AM-7, 2.0L, 4cyl	30	26/38	$1,900	8	P T SS
CLA45 AMG 4matic					
AM-7, 2.0L, 4cyl	26	23/31	$2,200	7	P T SS
CLS550					
A-7, 4.7L, 8cyl	21	18/27	$2,700	5	P T SS
CLS550 4matic					
A-7, 4.7L, 8cyl	20	18/25	$2,850	5	P T SS
CLS63 AMG					
A-7, 5.5L, 8cyl	19	16/25	$3,000	4	P T SS
CLS63 AMG 4matic					
A-7, 5.5L, 8cyl	18	16/22	$3,150	4	P T SS
CLS63 AMG S					
A-7, 5.5L, 8cyl	19	16/25	$3,000	4	P T SS
CLS63 AMG S 4matic					
A-7, 5.5L, 8cyl	18	16/22	$3,150	4	P T SS
MINI					
Cooper Countryman					
A-S6, 1.6L, 4cyl	27	25/30	$2,100	7	P
M-6, 1.6L, 4cyl	31	28/35	$1,850	8	P
Cooper Paceman					
A-S6, 1.6L, 4cyl	27	25/30	$2,100	7	P
M-6, 1.6L, 4cyl	31	28/35	$1,850	8	P
Cooper S Countryman					
A-S6, 1.6L, 4cyl	28	25/32	$2,000	7	P T
M-6, 1.6L, 4cyl	29	26/32	$1,950	7	P T
Cooper S Countryman All4					
A-S6, 1.6L, 4cyl	26	23/30	$2,200	7	P T
M-6, 1.6L, 4cyl	27	25/31	$2,100	7	P T
Cooper S Paceman					
A-S6, 1.6L, 4cyl	28	25/32	$2,000	7	P T
M-6, 1.6L, 4cyl	29	26/32	$1,950	7	P T
Cooper S Paceman All4					
A-S6, 1.6L, 4cyl	26	23/30	$2,200	7	P T
M-6, 1.6L, 4cyl	27	25/31	$2,100	7	P T
JCW Countryman All4					
A-S6, 1.6L, 4cyl	26	23/30	$2,200	7	P T
M-6, 1.6L, 4cyl	27	25/31	$2,100	7	P T
JCW Paceman All4					
A-S6, 1.6L, 4cyl	26	23/30	$2,200	7	P T
M-6, 1.6L, 4cyl	27	25/31	$2,100	7	P T
MITSUBISHI					
Lancer					
AM-6, 2.0L, 4cyl	20	18/25	$2,850	5	P T
AV-S6, 2.0L, 4cyl	29	26/34	$1,800	7	
M-5, 2.0L, 4cyl	28	25/34	$1,850	7	
AV-S6, 2.4L, 4cyl	26	23/30	$2,000	7	
M-5, 2.4L, 4cyl	26	22/31	$2,000	7	
Lancer AWD					
AV-S6, 2.4L, 4cyl	25	22/29	$2,050	6	
Lancer Evolution					
AM-6, 2.0L, 4cyl	19	17/22	$3,000	4	P T
M-5, 2.0L, 4cyl	19	17/23	$3,000	4	P T
Mirage					
AV, 1.2L, 3cyl	40	37/44	$1,300	9	
M-5, 1.2L, 3cyl	37	34/42	$1,400	9	
NISSAN					
Versa					
AV, 1.6L, 4cyl	35	31/40	$1,500	9	
A-4, 1.6L, 4cyl	30	26/35	$1,700	8	
M-5, 1.6L, 4cyl	30	27/36	$1,700	8	
ROLLS-ROYCE					
Phantom Coupe					
A-S8, 6.7L, 12cyl	14	11/19	$4,050	2	P Tax

Manufacturer Model Configuration (trans, eng size, cyl)	MPG		Annual Fuel Cost	GHG Rating	Notes
	Comb	City/Hwy			

Phantom Drophead Coupe

	Comb	City/Hwy	Annual Fuel Cost	GHG Rating	Notes
A-S8, 6.7L, 12cyl	14	11/19	$4,050	2	P Tax

SCION

tC

	Comb	City/Hwy	Annual Fuel Cost	GHG Rating	Notes
A-S6, 2.5L, 4cyl	26	23/31	$2,000	7	
M-6, 2.5L, 4cyl	26	23/31	$2,000	7	

SUBARU

Impreza AWD

	Comb	City/Hwy	Annual Fuel Cost	GHG Rating	Notes
AV, 2.0L, 4cyl	30	27/36	$1,700	8	
M-5, 2.0L, 4cyl	28	25/34	$1,850	7	
M-5, 2.5L, 4cyl	21	19/25	$2,700	5	P T
M-6, 2.5L, 4cyl	19	17/23	$3,000	4	P T

TOYOTA

Prius c

	Comb	City/Hwy	Annual Fuel Cost	GHG Rating	Notes
▶ AV, 1.5L, 4cyl	50	53/46	$1,050	10	HEV SS

Yaris

	Comb	City/Hwy	Annual Fuel Cost	GHG Rating	Notes
A-4, 1.5L, 4cyl	32	30/36	$1,600	8	
M-5, 1.5L, 4cyl	33	30/37	$1,550	8	

VOLKSWAGEN

Beetle

	Comb	City/Hwy	Annual Fuel Cost	GHG Rating	Notes
A-S6, 1.8L, 4cyl	28	25/33	$1,850	7	T
M-5, 1.8L, 4cyl	27	24/33	$1,900	7	T
AM-S6, 2.0L, 4cyl	26	24/30	$2,200	7	P T
M-6, 2.0L, 4cyl	26	23/31	$2,200	7	P T
A-S6, 2.5L, 5cyl	25	22/29	$2,050	6	
M-5, 2.5L, 5cyl	25	22/31	$2,050	6	
AM-S6, 2.0L, 4cyl	32	29/39	$1,900	7	D T
M-6, 2.0L, 4cyl	32	28/41	$1,900	7	D T

CC

	Comb	City/Hwy	Annual Fuel Cost	GHG Rating	Notes
AM-S6, 2.0L, 4cyl	25	22/31	$2,250	6	P T
M-6, 2.0L, 4cyl	25	21/32	$2,250	6	P T

CC 4motion

	Comb	City/Hwy	Annual Fuel Cost	GHG Rating	Notes
A-S6, 3.6L, 6cyl	20	17/25	$2,850	5	P

Golf

	Comb	City/Hwy	Annual Fuel Cost	GHG Rating	Notes
A-S6, 2.5L, 5cyl	26	23/30	$2,000	7	
AM-S6, 2.0L, 4cyl	34	30/42	$1,750	8	D T
M-6, 2.0L, 4cyl	34	30/42	$1,750	8	D T

GTI

	Comb	City/Hwy	Annual Fuel Cost	GHG Rating	Notes
AM-S6, 2.0L, 4cyl	27	24/32	$2,100	7	P T
M-6, 2.0L, 4cyl	25	21/31	$2,250	6	P T

Jetta

	Comb	City/Hwy	Annual Fuel Cost	GHG Rating	Notes
A-S6, 1.8L, 4cyl	29	25/36	$1,800	7	T
M-5, 1.8L, 4cyl	30	26/36	$1,700	8	T
AM-S6, 2.0L, 4cyl	27	24/32	$2,100	7	P T
A-S6, 2.0L, 4cyl	25	23/29	$2,050	6	
M-5, 2.0L, 4cyl	28	24/34	$1,850	7	
M-6, 2.0L, 4cyl	26	23/33	$2,200	7	P T
AM-S6, 2.0L, 4cyl	34	30/42	$1,750	8	D T
M-6, 2.0L, 4cyl	34	30/42	$1,750	8	D T

Jetta Hybrid

	Comb	City/Hwy	Annual Fuel Cost	GHG Rating	Notes
AM-S7, 1.4L, 4cyl	45	42/48	$1,250	10	P T HEV SS

VOLVO

S60 AWD

	Comb	City/Hwy	Annual Fuel Cost	GHG Rating	Notes
A-S6, 2.5L, 5cyl	23	20/29	$2,250	6	T
A-S6, 3.0L, 6cyl	21	18/25	$2,450	5	T

S60 FWD

	Comb	City/Hwy	Annual Fuel Cost	GHG Rating	Notes
A-S6, 2.5L, 5cyl	24	21/30	$2,150	6	T

MIDSIZE CARS

ACURA

RLX

	Comb	City/Hwy	Annual Fuel Cost	GHG Rating	Notes
A-S6, 3.5L, 6cyl	24	20/31	$2,350	6	P

RLX Hybrid

	Comb	City/Hwy	Annual Fuel Cost	GHG Rating	Notes
A-S7, 3.5L, 6cyl	30	28/32	$1,900	8	P HEV SS

TL 2WD

	Comb	City/Hwy	Annual Fuel Cost	GHG Rating	Notes
A-S6, 3.5L, 6cyl	23	20/29	$2,450	6	P

TL 4WD

	Comb	City/Hwy	Annual Fuel Cost	GHG Rating	Notes
A-S6, 3.7L, 6cyl	21	18/26	$2,700	5	P
M-6, 3.7L, 6cyl	20	17/25	$2,850	5	P

AUDI

A6

	Comb	City/Hwy	Annual Fuel Cost	GHG Rating	Notes
AV-S8, 2.0L, 4cyl	28	25/33	$2,000	7	P T

A6 quattro

	Comb	City/Hwy	Annual Fuel Cost	GHG Rating	Notes
A-S8, 2.0L, 4cyl	23	20/29	$2,450	6	P T
A-S8, 3.0L, 6cyl	22	18/27	$2,600	5	P S
A-S8, 3.0L, 6cyl	29	24/38	$2,100	7	D T SS

A7 quattro

	Comb	City/Hwy	Annual Fuel Cost	GHG Rating	Notes
A-S8, 3.0L, 6cyl	21	18/28	$2,700	5	P S SS
A-S8, 3.0L, 6cyl	29	24/38	$2,100	7	D T SS

A8

	Comb	City/Hwy	Annual Fuel Cost	GHG Rating	Notes
A-S8, 3.0L, 6cyl	21	18/28	$2,700	5	P S SS
A-S8, 4.0L, 8cyl	21	17/28	$2,700	5	P T SS

RS 7

	Comb	City/Hwy	Annual Fuel Cost	GHG Rating	Notes
A-S8, 4.0L, 8cyl	19	16/27	$3,000	4	P T

S6

	Comb	City/Hwy	Annual Fuel Cost	GHG Rating	Notes
AM-S7, 4.0L, 8cyl	20	17/27	$2,850	5	P T

S7

	Comb	City/Hwy	Annual Fuel Cost	GHG Rating	Notes
AM-S7, 4.0L, 8cyl	20	17/27	$2,850	5	P T

S8

	Comb	City/Hwy	Annual Fuel Cost	GHG Rating	Notes
A-S8, 4.0L, 8cyl	19	15/26	$3,000	4	P T

BENTLEY

Flying Spur

	Comb	City/Hwy	Annual Fuel Cost	GHG Rating	Notes
A-S8, 6.0L, 12cyl	15	12/20	$3,800	2	Gas P T Tax
	11	9/15	$4,150	2	E85

Mulsanne

	Comb	City/Hwy	Annual Fuel Cost	GHG Rating	Notes
A-S8, 6.8L, 8cyl	13	11/18	$4,350	1	P T Tax

BMW

528i

	Comb	City/Hwy	Annual Fuel Cost	GHG Rating	Notes
A-S8, 2.0L, 4cyl	27	23/34	$2,100	7	P T SS

528i xDrive

	Comb	City/Hwy	Annual Fuel Cost	GHG Rating	Notes
A-S8, 2.0L, 4cyl	26	22/33	$2,200	7	P T SS

535d

	Comb	City/Hwy	Annual Fuel Cost	GHG Rating	Notes
A-S8, 3.0L, 6cyl	30	26/38	$2,000	7	D T

535d xDrive

	Comb	City/Hwy	Annual Fuel Cost	GHG Rating	Notes
A-S8, 3.0L, 6cyl	30	26/37	$2,000	7	D T

535i

	Comb	City/Hwy	Annual Fuel Cost	GHG Rating	Notes
A-S8, 3.0L, 6cyl	24	20/30	$2,350	6	P T SS
M-6, 3.0L, 6cyl	23	20/30	$2,450	6	P T SS

535i xDrive

	Comb	City/Hwy	Annual Fuel Cost	GHG Rating	Notes
A-S8, 3.0L, 6cyl	23	20/29	$2,450	6	P T SS

Manufacturer Model Configuration (trans, eng size, cyl)	MPG Comb	MPG City/Hwy	Annual Fuel Cost	GHG Rating	Notes
550i					
A-S8, 4.4L, 8cyl	20	17/25	$2,850	5	P T SS
550i xDrive					
A-S8, 4.4L, 8cyl	19	16/24	$3,000	4	P T
ActiveHybrid 5					
A-S8, 3.0L, 6cyl	26	23/30	$2,200	7	P T HEV SS
M5					
AM-S7, 4.4L, 8cyl	16	14/20	$3,550	3	P T Tax SS
M-6, 4.4L, 8cyl	17	15/22	$3,350	3	P T Tax SS
BUICK					
LaCrosse					
A-S6, 3.6L, 6cyl	21	18/28	$2,450	5	
A-S6, 3.6L, 6cyl	21	18/28	$2,450	5	Gas
	16	14/20	$2,850	6	E85
LaCrosse AWD					
A-S6, 3.6L, 6cyl	20	17/26	$2,600	5	Gas
	14	12/18	$3,250	5	E85
LaCrosse eAssist					
A-S6, 2.4L, 4cyl	29	25/36	$1,800	7	HEV SS
Regal					
A-S6, 2.0L, 4cyl	24	21/30	$2,150	6	T
M-6, 2.0L, 4cyl	24	20/31	$2,150	6	T
A-S6, 2.4L, 4cyl	23	19/31	$2,250	6	
Regal AWD					
A-S6, 2.0L, 4cyl	22	19/27	$2,350	5	T
Regal eAssist					
A-S6, 2.4L, 4cyl	29	25/36	$1,800	7	HEV SS
CADILLAC					
CTS					
A-S6, 3.6L, 6cyl	21	18/27	$2,450	5	
A-S6, 6.2L, 8cyl	14	12/18	$4,050	2	P S Tax
M-6, 6.2L, 8cyl	16	14/19	$3,550	3	P S Tax
CTS AWD					
A-S6, 3.6L, 6cyl	21	18/26	$2,450	5	
CTS Sedan					
A-S6, 2.0L, 4cyl	23	20/30	$2,250	6	T
A-S8, 3.6L, 6cyl	22	18/29	$2,350	5	
A-S8, 3.6L, 6cyl	18	16/24	$3,150	4	P T
CTS Sedan AWD					
A-S6, 2.0L, 4cyl	22	19/28	$2,350	5	T
A-S6, 3.6L, 6cyl	21	18/26	$2,450	5	
CTS V					
A-S6, 6.2L, 8cyl	14	12/18	$4,050	2	P S Tax
M-6, 6.2L, 8cyl	16	14/19	$3,550	3	P S Tax
CHEVROLET					
Cruze					
A-S6, 1.4L, 4cyl	30	26/38	$1,700	8	T
M-6, 1.4L, 4cyl	30	26/38	$1,700	8	T
A-S6, 1.8L, 4cyl	27	22/35	$1,900	7	
M-6, 1.8L, 4cyl	29	25/36	$1,800	7	
A-S6, 2.0L, 4cyl	33	27/46	$1,850	7	D T
Cruze Eco					
A-6, 1.4L, 4cyl	31	26/39	$1,650	8	T
M-6, 1.4L, 4cyl	33	28/42	$1,550	8	T
Malibu					
A-S6, 2.0L, 4cyl	24	21/30	$2,150	6	T
A-S6, 2.5L, 4cyl	29	25/36	$1,800	7	SS
Malibu eAssist					
A-S6, 2.4L, 4cyl	29	25/36	$1,800	7	HEV SS
Sonic 5					
A-S6, 1.4L, 4cyl	31	27/37	$1,650	8	T
M-6, 1.4L, 4cyl	33	29/40	$1,550	8	T
A-S6, 1.8L, 4cyl	28	25/35	$1,850	7	
M-5, 1.8L, 4cyl	30	26/35	$1,700	8	
Sonic 5 RS					
A-S6, 1.4L, 4cyl	28	25/33	$1,850	7	T
M-6, 1.4L, 4cyl	30	27/34	$1,700	8	T
CHRYSLER					
200					
A-4, 2.4L, 4cyl	24	21/30	$2,150	6	
A-6, 2.4L, 4cyl	24	20/31	$2,150	6	
A-6, 3.6L, 6cyl	22	19/29	$2,350	5	Gas
	16	14/21	$2,850	6	E85
DODGE					
Avenger					
A-4, 2.4L, 4cyl	24	21/30	$2,150	6	
A-6, 2.4L, 4cyl	24	20/31	$2,150	6	
A-6, 3.6L, 6cyl	22	19/29	$2,350	5	Gas
	16	14/21	$2,850	6	E85
Challenger					
A-5, 3.6L, 6cyl	21	18/27	$2,600	5	Mid
A-5, 5.7L, 8cyl	18	15/25	$3,000	4	Mid
M-6, 5.7L, 8cyl	18	15/23	$3,150	4	P
Challenger SRT8					
A-5, 6.4L, 8cyl	17	14/23	$3,350	3	P Tax
M-6, 6.4L, 8cyl	17	14/23	$3,350	3	P Tax
Dart					
M-6, 2.0L, 4cyl	29	25/36	$1,800	7	
A-6, 2.4L, 4cyl	27	23/35	$1,900	7	
M-6, 2.4L, 4cyl	27	22/35	$1,900	7	
A-6, 2.0L, 4cyl	27	24/34	$1,900	7	Gas
	19	17/24	$2,400	7	E85
Dart Aero					
AM-6, 1.4L, 4cyl	32	28/40	$1,800	8	P T
M-6, 1.4L, 4cyl	32	28/41	$1,800	8	P T
Dart GT					
A-6, 2.4L, 4cyl	26	22/31	$2,000	7	
M-6, 2.4L, 4cyl	27	23/33	$1,900	7	
FERRARI					
FF					
AM-7, 6.3L, 12cyl	13	11/17	$4,350	1	P Tax PT4WD SS
AM-7, 6.3L, 12cyl	13	11/16	$4,350	1	P Tax PT4WD
FORD					
C-MAX Energi Plug-in Hybrid					
▶ AV, 2.0L, 4cyl		See page 34			PHEV SS
Fusion AWD					
A-S6, 2.0L, 4cyl	25	22/31	$2,050	6	T

Manufacturer Model Configuration (trans, eng size, cyl)	MPG Comb	MPG City/Hwy	Annual Fuel Cost	GHG Rating	Notes
Fusion Energi Plug-in Hybrid					
AV, 2.0L, 4cyl		See page 34			PHEV SS
Fusion FWD					
A-S6, 1.5L, 4cyl	29	25/37	$1,800	7	T SS
A-S6, 1.5L, 4cyl	28	23/36	$1,850	7	T
M-6, 1.6L, 4cyl	29	25/37	$1,800	7	T
A-S6, 2.0L, 4cyl	26	22/33	$2,000	7	T
A-S6, 2.5L, 4cyl	26	22/34	$2,000	7	
Fusion Hybrid FWD					
AV, 2.0L, 4cyl	47	47/47	$1,100	10	HEV SS
HONDA					
Accord					
AV-S7, 2.4L, 4cyl	29	26/34	$1,800	7	
AV, 2.4L, 4cyl	30	27/36	$1,700	8	
M-6, 2.4L, 4cyl	28	24/34	$1,850	7	
A-S6, 3.5L, 6cyl	25	21/32	$2,050	6	
A-6, 3.5L, 6cyl	26	21/34	$2,000	7	
M-6, 3.5L, 6cyl	22	18/28	$2,350	5	
Accord Hybrid					
AV, 2.0L, 4cyl	47	50/45	$1,100	10	HEV SS
Accord Plug-in Hybrid					
AV, 2.0L, 4cyl		See page 34			PHEV SS
HYUNDAI					
Elantra					
A-6, 1.8L, 4cyl	32	28/38	$1,600	8	
M-6, 1.8L, 4cyl	31	27/37	$1,650	8	
A-6, 2.0L, 4cyl	28	24/35	$1,850	7	
M-6, 2.0L, 4cyl	28	24/34	$1,850	7	
Elantra Coupe					
A-6, 2.0L, 4cyl	28	24/34	$1,850	7	
Elantra GT					
A-6, 2.0L, 4cyl	27	24/33	$1,900	7	
M-6, 2.0L, 4cyl	28	24/34	$1,850	7	
Elantra Limited					
A-6, 1.8L, 4cyl	31	27/37	$1,650	8	
Sonata Hybrid					
AM-6, 2.4L, 4cyl	38	36/40	$1,350	9	HEV SS
Sonata Hybrid Limited					
AM-6, 2.4L, 4cyl	37	36/40	$1,400	9	HEV SS
INFINITI					
Q50					
A-S7, 3.7L, 6cyl	23	20/29	$2,450	6	P
Q50 AWD					
A-S7, 3.7L, 6cyl	22	19/27	$2,600	5	P
Q50a					
A-S7, 3.7L, 6cyl	23	20/30	$2,450	6	P
Q50a AWD					
A-S7, 3.7L, 6cyl	22	19/27	$2,600	5	P
Q70					
A-S7, 3.7L, 6cyl	21	18/26	$2,700	5	P
A-S7, 5.6L, 8cyl	19	16/24	$3,000	4	P
Q70 AWD					
A-S7, 3.7L, 6cyl	20	17/24	$2,850	5	P
A-S7, 5.6L, 8cyl	18	16/23	$3,150	4	P

Manufacturer Model Configuration (trans, eng size, cyl)	MPG Comb	MPG City/Hwy	Annual Fuel Cost	GHG Rating	Notes
Q70 Hybrid					
A-S7, 3.5L, 6cyl	31	29/34	$1,850	8	P HEV SS
JAGUAR					
XF					
A-S8, 2.0L, 4cyl	23	19/30	$2,450	6	P T
A-S8, 5.0L, 8cyl	18	15/23	$3,150	4	P S SS
XF AWD					
A-S8, 3.0L, 6cyl	19	16/26	$3,000	4	P S SS
XF FFV					
A-S8, 3.0L, 6cyl	21	17/28	$2,700	5	Gas P S SS
	15	13/19	$3,050	5	E85
A-S8, 5.0L, 8cyl	18	15/23	$3,150	4	Gas P S SS
	13	11/17	$3,500	4	E85
KIA					
Forte					
A-6, 1.8L, 4cyl	29	25/36	$1,800	7	
M-6, 1.8L, 4cyl	29	25/37	$1,800	7	
A-6, 2.0L, 4cyl	28	24/36	$1,850	7	
M-6, 2.0L, 4cyl	28	24/35	$1,850	7	
Forte Eco					
A-6, 1.8L, 4cyl	29	26/35	$1,800	7	
Optima					
A-6, 2.0L, 4cyl	24	20/31	$2,150	6	T
A-6, 2.4L, 4cyl	27	23/34	$1,900	7	
Optima Hybrid					
AM-6, 2.4L, 4cyl	38	36/40	$1,350	9	HEV SS
Optima Hybrid EX					
AM-6, 2.4L, 4cyl	37	35/39	$1,400	9	HEV SS
LEXUS					
ES 300h					
AV-S6, 2.5L, 4cyl	40	40/39	$1,300	9	HEV SS
ES 350					
A-S6, 3.5L, 6cyl	24	21/31	$2,150	6	
GS 350					
A-S8, 3.5L, 6cyl	23	19/29	$2,450	6	P
GS 350 AWD					
A-S6, 3.5L, 6cyl	21	19/26	$2,700	5	P
GS 450h					
AV-S8, 3.5L, 6cyl	31	29/34	$1,850	8	P HEV SS
LS 460					
A-S8, 4.6L, 8cyl	19	16/24	$3,000	4	P
LS 460 AWD					
A-S8, 4.6L, 8cyl	18	16/23	$3,150	4	P
LS 460 L					
A-S8, 4.6L, 8cyl	19	16/24	$3,000	4	P
LS 460 L AWD					
A-S8, 4.6L, 8cyl	18	16/23	$3,150	4	P
LS 600h L					
AV-S8, 5.0L, 8cyl	20	19/23	$2,850	5	P HEV SS

Manufacturer Model Configuration (trans, eng size, cyl)	MPG Comb	MPG City/Hwy	Annual Fuel Cost	GHG Rating	Notes
LINCOLN					
MKZ AWD					
A-S6, 2.0L, 4cyl	25	22/31	$2,050	6	T
A-S6, 3.7L, 6cyl	21	18/26	$2,450	5	
MKZ FWD					
A-S6, 2.0L, 4cyl	26	22/33	$2,000	7	T
A-S6, 3.7L, 6cyl	22	19/28	$2,350	5	
MKZ Hybrid FWD					
AV, 2.0L, 4cyl	45	45/45	$1,150	10	HEV SS
MASERATI					
Ghibli V6					
A-8, 3.0L, 6cyl	19	15/25	$3,000	4	P T
Ghibli V6 AWD					
A-8, 3.0L, 6cyl	18	15/25	$3,150	4	P T
MAZDA					
3 5-Door					
A-S6, 2.0L, 4cyl	33	30/40	$1,550	8	
M-6, 2.0L, 4cyl	33	29/40	$1,550	8	
A-S6, 2.5L, 4cyl	32	28/38	$1,600	8	i-ELOOP
A-S6, 2.5L, 4cyl	31	27/37	$1,650	8	
6					
A-S6, 2.5L, 4cyl	32	28/40	$1,600	8	i-ELOOP
A-S6, 2.5L, 4cyl	30	26/38	$1,700	8	
M-6, 2.5L, 4cyl	29	25/37	$1,800	7	
MERCEDES-BENZ					
E250 Bluetec					
A-7, 2.1L, 4cyl	34	28/45	$1,750	8	D T SS
E250 Bluetec 4matic					
A-7, 2.1L, 4cyl	32	27/42	$1,900	7	D T SS
E350					
A-7, 3.5L, 6cyl	24	21/30	$2,350	6	P SS
A-7, 3.5L, 6cyl	24	21/30	$2,350	6	P PZEV SS
A-7, 3.5L, 6cyl	24	21/31	$2,350	6	Gas P SS
	18	16/23	$2,550	6	E85
E350 4matic					
A-7, 3.5L, 6cyl	24	21/29	$2,350	6	P PZEV SS
A-7, 3.5L, 6cyl	23	20/28	$2,450	6	P SS
A-7, 3.5L, 6cyl	24	20/29	$2,350	6	Gas P SS
	17	15/21	$2,700	6	E85
E400 Hybrid					
A-7, 3.5L, 6cyl	26	24/30	$2,200	7	P HEV SS
E550 4matic					
A-7, 4.7L, 8cyl	20	17/26	$2,850	5	P T SS
E63 AMG					
A-7, 5.5L, 8cyl	19	16/24	$3,000	4	P T
E63 AMG 4matic					
A-7, 5.5L, 8cyl	18	16/23	$3,150	4	P T SS
E63 AMG S					
A-7, 5.5L, 8cyl	19	16/24	$3,000	4	P T
E63 AMG S 4matic					
A-7, 5.5L, 8cyl	18	16/23	$3,150	4	P T SS

Manufacturer Model Configuration (trans, eng size, cyl)	MPG Comb	MPG City/Hwy	Annual Fuel Cost	GHG Rating	Notes
NISSAN					
Altima					
AV, 2.5L, 4cyl	31	27/38	$1,650	8	
AV-S7, 3.5L, 6cyl	25	22/31	$2,050	6	
Leaf					
▶ A-1	114	126/101	$550	10	EV
Maxima					
AV-S6, 3.5L, 6cyl	22	19/26	$2,600	5	P
Sentra					
AV, 1.8L, 4cyl	34	30/39	$1,500	8	
AV, 1.8L, 4cyl	33	30/39	$1,550	8	
M-6, 1.8L, 4cyl	30	27/36	$1,700	8	
Sentra FE					
AV, 1.8L, 4cyl	34	30/40	$1,500	8	
ROLLS-ROYCE					
Wraith					
A-S8, 6.6L, 12cyl	15	13/21	$3,800	2	P T Tax
SUBARU					
Legacy AWD					
AV, 2.5L, 4cyl	27	24/32	$1,900	7	
M-6, 2.5L, 4cyl	24	21/29	$2,150	6	
A-S5, 3.6L, 6cyl	20	18/25	$2,600	5	
TOYOTA					
Avalon					
A-S6, 3.5L, 6cyl	24	21/31	$2,150	6	3 Mode
A-S6, 3.5L, 6cyl	25	21/31	$2,050	6	
Avalon Hybrid					
AV-S6, 2.5L, 4cyl	40	40/39	$1,300	9	HEV SS
Camry					
A-S6, 2.5L, 4cyl	28	25/35	$1,850	7	
A-S6, 3.5L, 6cyl	25	21/31	$2,050	6	
Camry Hybrid LE					
AV, 2.5L, 4cyl	41	43/39	$1,250	9	HEV SS
Camry Hybrid XLE/SE					
AV, 2.5L, 4cyl	40	40/38	$1,300	9	HEV SS
Corolla					
AV-S7, 1.8L, 4cyl	32	29/37	$1,600	8	
AV, 1.8L, 4cyl	32	29/38	$1,600	8	
A-4, 1.8L, 4cyl	31	27/36	$1,650	8	
M-6, 1.8L, 4cyl	31	28/37	$1,650	8	
Corolla LE Eco					
AV, 1.8L, 4cyl	35	30/42	$1,500	9	
AV, 1.8L, 4cyl	34	30/40	$1,500	8	2 mode
Prius					
▶ AV, 1.8L, 4cyl	50	51/48	$1,050	10	HEV SS
Prius Plug-in Hybrid					
▶ AV, 1.8L, 4cyl		See page 34			PHEV SS

Manufacturer Model Configuration (trans, eng size, cyl)	MPG		Annual Fuel Cost	GHG Rating	Notes
	Comb	City/Hwy			
VOLKSWAGEN					
Passat					
A-S6, 1.8L, 4cyl	28	24/34	$1,850	7	T
M-5, 1.8L, 4cyl	28	24/35	$1,850	7	T
A-S6, 2.5L, 5cyl	25	22/31	$2,050	6	
M-5, 2.5L, 5cyl	26	22/32	$2,000	7	
AM-S6, 3.6L, 6cyl	23	20/28	$2,450	6	P
AM-S6, 2.0L, 4cyl	34	30/40	$1,750	8	D T
M-6, 2.0L, 4cyl	35	31/43	$1,750	8	D T
VOLVO					
S80 AWD					
A-S6, 3.0L, 6cyl	21	18/25	$2,450	5	T
S80 FWD					
A-S6, 3.2L, 6cyl	23	20/29	$2,250	6	

LARGE CARS

Manufacturer Model Configuration (trans, eng size, cyl)	MPG		Annual Fuel Cost	GHG Rating	Notes
	Comb	City/Hwy			
AUDI					
A8 L					
A-S8, 3.0L, 6cyl	21	18/28	$2,700	5	P S SS
A-S8, 4.0L, 8cyl	19	16/26	$3,000	4	P T SS
A-S8, 6.3L, 12cyl	16	13/21	$3,550	3	P Tax
A-S8, 3.0L, 6cyl	28	24/36	$2,150	6	D T SS
BMW					
328i xDrive Gran Turismo					
A-S8, 2.0L, 4cyl	26	22/33	$2,200	7	P T SS
335i xDrive Gran Turismo					
A-S8, 3.0L, 6cyl	24	20/30	$2,350	6	P T SS
535i Gran Turismo					
A-S8, 3.0L, 6cyl	22	19/28	$2,600	5	P T SS
535i xDrive Gran Turismo					
A-S8, 3.0L, 6cyl	21	18/26	$2,700	5	P T SS
550i Gran Turismo					
A-S8, 4.4L, 8cyl	19	16/25	$3,000	4	P T SS
550i xDrive Gran Turismo					
A-S8, 4.4L, 8cyl	19	16/24	$3,000	4	P T SS
740i					
A-S8, 3.0L, 6cyl	22	19/29	$2,600	5	P T SS
740Li					
A-S8, 3.0L, 6cyl	22	19/29	$2,600	5	P T SS
740Li xDrive					
A-S8, 3.0L, 6cyl	22	19/28	$2,600	5	P T SS
750i					
A-S8, 4.4L, 8cyl	20	17/25	$2,850	5	P T SS
750i xDrive					
A-S8, 4.4L, 8cyl	19	16/24	$3,000	4	P T SS
750Li					
A-S8, 4.4L, 8cyl	19	16/25	$3,000	4	P T SS
750Li xDrive					
A-S8, 4.4L, 8cyl	19	16/24	$3,000	4	P T SS
760Li					
A-S8, 6.0L, 12cyl	15	13/20	$3,800	2	P T Tax
ActiveHybrid 7L					
A-S8, 3.0L, 6cyl	25	22/30	$2,250	6	P T HEV SS

Manufacturer Model Configuration (trans, eng size, cyl)	MPG		Annual Fuel Cost	GHG Rating	Notes
	Comb	City/Hwy			
Alpina B7 LWB					
A-S8, 4.4L, 8cyl	19	16/25	$3,000	4	P T SS
Alpina B7 LWB xDrive					
A-S8, 4.4L, 8cyl	19	16/24	$3,000	4	P T SS
Alpina B7 SWB					
A-S8, 4.4L, 8cyl	19	16/25	$3,000	4	P T SS
Alpina B7 SWB xDrive					
A-S8, 4.4L, 8cyl	19	16/24	$3,000	4	P T SS
X1 sDrive28i					
A-S8, 2.0L, 4cyl	27	23/34	$2,100	7	P T SS
X1 xDrive28i					
A-S8, 2.0L, 4cyl	26	22/33	$2,200	7	P T SS
X1 xDrive35i					
A-S6, 3.0L, 6cyl	21	18/27	$2,700	5	P T
CADILLAC					
XTS					
A-S6, 3.6L, 6cyl	21	18/28	$2,450	5	
XTS AWD					
A-S6, 3.6L, 6cyl	20	17/26	$2,600	5	
A-S6, 3.6L, 6cyl	19	16/24	$3,000	4	P T
CHEVROLET					
Impala					
A-S6, 2.5L, 4cyl	25	21/31	$2,050	6	
A-S6, 3.6L, 6cyl	21	18/28	$2,450	5	
A-S6, 3.6L, 6cyl	22	19/29	$2,350	5	Gas
	16	14/20	$2,850	6	E85
Impala eAssist					
A-S6, 2.4L, 4cyl	29	25/35	$1,800	7	HEV SS
Impala Limited					
A-6, 3.6L, 6cyl	22	18/30	$2,350	5	Gas
	16	13/22	$2,850	6	E85
SS					
A-S6, 6.2L, 8cyl	17	14/21	$3,050	3	Tax
CHRYSLER					
300					
A-8, 3.6L, 6cyl	23	19/31	$2,250	6	
A-5, 5.7L, 8cyl	18	15/25	$3,000	4	Mid
A-8, 3.6L, 6cyl	23	19/31	$2,250	6	Gas
	17	14/23	$2,700	6	E85
300 AWD					
A-8, 3.6L, 6cyl	21	18/27	$2,450	5	
A-5, 5.7L, 8cyl	18	15/23	$3,000	4	Mid
A-8, 3.6L, 6cyl	21	18/27	$2,450	5	Gas
	16	14/20	$2,850	6	E85
300 SRT8					
A-5, 6.4L, 8cyl	17	14/23	$3,350	3	P Tax

DODGE

Manufacturer Model Configuration (trans, eng size, cyl)	Comb	City/Hwy	Annual Fuel Cost	GHG Rating	Notes
Charger					
A-5, 3.6L, 6cyl	21	18/27	$2,450	5	
A-8, 3.6L, 6cyl	23	19/31	$2,250	6	
A-5, 5.7L, 8cyl	18	15/25	$3,000	4	Mid
A-5, 3.6L, 6cyl	21	18/27	$2,450	5	Gas
	15	13/19	$3,050	5	E85
A-8, 3.6L, 6cyl	23	19/31	$2,250	6	Gas
	17	14/23	$2,700	6	E85
Charger AWD					
A-8, 3.6L, 6cyl	21	18/27	$2,450	5	
A-5, 5.7L, 8cyl	18	15/23	$3,000	4	Mid
A-8, 3.6L, 6cyl	21	18/27	$2,450	5	Gas
	16	14/20	$2,850	6	E85
Charger SRT8					
A-5, 6.4L, 8cyl	17	14/23	$3,350	3	P Tax

FORD

Manufacturer Model Configuration (trans, eng size, cyl)	Comb	City/Hwy	Annual Fuel Cost	GHG Rating	Notes
C-MAX Hybrid FWD					
▶ AV, 2.0L, 4cyl	43	45/40	$1,200	10	HEV SS
Special Service Police FWD					
A-6, 2.0L, 4cyl	24	20/30	$2,150	6	T
Taurus AWD					
A-S6, 3.5L, 6cyl	21	18/26	$2,450	5	
A-S6, 3.5L, 6cyl	20	17/25	$2,600	5	T
Taurus AWD FFV					
A-S6, 3.5L, 6cyl	21	18/26	$2,450	5	Gas
	15	13/19	$3,050	5	E85
Taurus FWD					
A-S6, 2.0L, 4cyl	26	22/32	$2,000	7	T
A-S6, 3.5L, 6cyl	23	19/29	$2,250	6	
Taurus FWD FFV					
A-S6, 3.5L, 6cyl	23	19/29	$2,250	6	Gas
	16	13/21	$2,850	6	E85

HYUNDAI

Manufacturer Model Configuration (trans, eng size, cyl)	Comb	City/Hwy	Annual Fuel Cost	GHG Rating	Notes
Azera					
A-6, 3.3L, 6cyl	23	19/29	$2,250	6	
Equus					
A-8, 5.0L, 8cyl	18	15/23	$3,150	4	P
Genesis					
A-8, 3.8L, 6cyl	21	18/27	$2,450	5	
Genesis R Spec					
A-8, 5.0L, 8cyl	18	15/23	$3,150	4	P
Sonata					
A-6, 2.0L, 4cyl	25	21/32	$2,050	6	T
A-6, 2.4L, 4cyl	28	24/35	$1,850	7	

JAGUAR

Manufacturer Model Configuration (trans, eng size, cyl)	Comb	City/Hwy	Annual Fuel Cost	GHG Rating	Notes
XJ					
A-S8, 5.0L, 8cyl	18	15/23	$3,150	4	P S SS
XJ AWD					
A-S8, 3.0L, 6cyl	19	16/24	$3,000	4	P S SS
XJ FFV					
A-S8, 3.0L, 6cyl	21	18/27	$2,700	5	Gas P S SS
	14	12/19	$3,250	5	E85
A-S8, 5.0L, 8cyl	18	15/23	$3,150	4	Gas P S SS
	13	11/17	$3,500	4	E85
XJL					
A-S8, 5.0L, 8cyl	18	15/23	$3,150	4	P S SS
XJL AWD					
A-S8, 3.0L, 6cyl	19	16/24	$3,000	4	P S SS
XJL FFV					
A-S8, 3.0L, 6cyl	20	17/27	$2,850	5	Gas P S SS
	14	11/19	$3,250	5	E85
A-S8, 5.0L, 8cyl	18	15/23	$3,150	4	Gas P S SS
	13	11/17	$3,500	4	E85

KIA

Manufacturer Model Configuration (trans, eng size, cyl)	Comb	City/Hwy	Annual Fuel Cost	GHG Rating	Notes
Cadenza					
A-6, 3.3L, 6cyl	22	19/28	$2,350	5	
Forte 5					
A-6, 1.6L, 4cyl	24	21/29	$2,150	6	T
M-6, 1.6L, 4cyl	24	21/29	$2,150	6	T
A-6, 2.0L, 4cyl	28	24/34	$1,850	7	
M-6, 2.0L, 4cyl	28	24/34	$1,850	7	

LINCOLN

Manufacturer Model Configuration (trans, eng size, cyl)	Comb	City/Hwy	Annual Fuel Cost	GHG Rating	Notes
MKS AWD					
A-S6, 3.5L, 6cyl	20	17/25	$2,600	5	T
A-S6, 3.7L, 6cyl	21	18/26	$2,450	5	
MKS FWD					
A-S6, 3.7L, 6cyl	22	19/28	$2,350	5	

MASERATI

Manufacturer Model Configuration (trans, eng size, cyl)	Comb	City/Hwy	Annual Fuel Cost	GHG Rating	Notes
Quattroporte GTS					
A-8, 3.8L, 8cyl	16	13/22	$3,550	3	P T Tax
Quattroporte SQ4 V6					
A-8, 3.0L, 6cyl	18	15/24	$3,150	4	P T

MERCEDES-BENZ

Manufacturer Model Configuration (trans, eng size, cyl)	Comb	City/Hwy	Annual Fuel Cost	GHG Rating	Notes
S550					
A-7, 4.7L, 8cyl	20	17/25	$2,850	5	P T SS
S550 4matic					
A-7, 4.7L, 8cyl	19	16/26	$3,000	4	P T SS
S63 AMG 4matic					
A-7, 5.5L, 8cyl	18	15/23	$3,150	4	P T SS

PORSCHE

Manufacturer Model Configuration (trans, eng size, cyl)	Comb	City/Hwy	Annual Fuel Cost	GHG Rating	Notes
Panamera					
AM-S7, 3.6L, 6cyl	22	18/28	$2,600	5	P SS
Panamera 4					
AM-S7, 3.6L, 6cyl	21	18/27	$2,700	5	P SS
Panamera 4S					
AM-S7, 3.0L, 6cyl	21	17/27	$2,700	5	P T SS
Panamera 4S Executive					
AM-S7, 3.0L, 6cyl	20	17/26	$2,850	5	P T SS
Panamera GTS					
AM-S7, 4.8L, 8cyl	19	16/24	$3,000	4	P SS

Manufacturer Model Configuration (trans, eng size, cyl)	MPG Comb	MPG City/Hwy	Annual Fuel Cost	GHG Rating	Notes
Panamera S					
AM-S7, 3.0L, 6cyl	21	17/27	$2,700	5	P T SS
Panamera Turbo					
AM-S7, 4.8L, 8cyl	18	15/24	$3,150	4	P T SS
Panamera Turbo Executive					
AM-S7, 4.8L, 8cyl	18	15/24	$3,150	4	P T SS
Panamera Turbo S					
AM-S7, 4.8L, 8cyl	18	15/24	$3,150	4	P T SS
Panamera Turbo S Executive					
AM-S7, 4.8L, 8cyl	18	15/24	$3,150	4	P T SS
ROLLS-ROYCE					
Ghost					
A-S8, 6.6L, 12cyl	15	13/21	$3,800	2	P T Tax
Ghost EWB					
A-S8, 6.6L, 12cyl	15	13/21	$3,800	2	P T Tax
Phantom					
A-S8, 6.7L, 12cyl	14	11/19	$4,050	2	P Tax
Phantom EWB					
A-S8, 6.7L, 12cyl	14	11/19	$4,050	2	P Tax

SMALL STATION WAGONS

Manufacturer Model Configuration (trans, eng size, cyl)	MPG Comb	MPG City/Hwy	Annual Fuel Cost	GHG Rating	Notes
ACURA					
TSX Wagon					
A-S5, 2.4L, 4cyl	25	22/30	$2,250	6	P
AUDI					
allroad quattro					
A-S8, 2.0L, 4cyl	23	20/27	$2,450	6	Gas P T
	15	14/18	$3,050	5	E85
BMW					
328d xDrive Sports Wagon					
A-S8, 2.0L, 4cyl	**35**	**31/43**	**$1,750**	**8**	**D T**
328i xDrive Sports Wagon					
A-S8, 2.0L, 4cyl	26	22/33	$2,200	7	P T SS
CADILLAC					
CTS Wagon					
A-S6, 3.0L, 6cyl	21	18/26	$2,450	5	
A-S6, 3.6L, 6cyl	21	18/26	$2,450	5	
A-S6, 6.2L, 8cyl	14	12/18	$4,050	2	P S Tax
M-6, 6.2L, 8cyl	16	14/19	$3,550	3	P S Tax
CTS Wagon AWD					
A-S6, 3.0L, 6cyl	21	18/26	$2,450	5	
A-S6, 3.6L, 6cyl	21	18/26	$2,450	5	
FIAT					
500 L					
A-6, 1.4L, 4cyl	27	24/33	$2,100	7	P T
M-6, 1.4L, 4cyl	28	25/33	$2,000	7	P T
HONDA					
Fit EV					
A-1	**118**	**132/105**	**$500**	**10**	**EV**
INFINITI					
QX50					
A-S7, 3.7L, 6cyl	20	17/25	$2,850	5	P
QX50 AWD					
A-S7, 3.7L, 6cyl	20	17/24	$2,850	5	P
KIA					
Soul					
A-6, 1.6L, 4cyl	26	24/30	$2,000	7	
M-6, 1.6L, 4cyl	26	24/30	$2,000	7	
A-6, 2.0L, 4cyl	26	23/31	$2,000	7	
Soul ECO dynamics					
A-6, 2.0L, 4cyl	27	24/31	$1,900	7	
MITSUBISHI					
Lancer Sportback					
AV-S6, 2.0L, 4cyl	27	24/32	$1,900	7	
AV-S6, 2.4L, 4cyl	25	22/29	$2,050	6	
NISSAN					
Cube					
AV, 1.8L, 4cyl	28	27/31	$1,850	7	
M-6, 1.8L, 4cyl	27	25/30	$1,900	7	
Juke					
AV-S6, 1.6L, 4cyl	29	27/32	$1,950	7	P T
M-6, 1.6L, 4cyl	27	25/31	$2,100	7	P T
Juke AWD					
AV-S6, 1.6L, 4cyl	27	25/30	$2,100	7	P T
SCION					
xB					
A-S4, 2.4L, 4cyl	24	22/28	$2,150	6	
M-5, 2.4L, 4cyl	24	22/28	$2,150	6	
SUBARU					
Impreza Wagon AWD					
AV, 2.0L, 4cyl	30	27/36	$1,700	8	
M-5, 2.0L, 4cyl	28	25/33	$1,850	7	
M-5, 2.5L, 4cyl	21	19/25	$2,700	5	P T
M-6, 2.5L, 4cyl	19	17/23	$3,000	4	P T
VOLKSWAGEN					
Jetta SportWagen					
A-S6, 2.5L, 5cyl	26	23/30	$2,000	7	
M-5, 2.5L, 5cyl	26	23/33	$2,000	7	
AM-S6, 2.0L, 4cyl	33	29/39	$1,850	7	D T
M-6, 2.0L, 4cyl	34	30/42	$1,750	8	D T

MIDSIZE STATION WAGONS

Manufacturer Model Configuration (trans, eng size, cyl)	MPG Comb	MPG City/Hwy	Annual Fuel Cost	GHG Rating	Notes
MERCEDES-BENZ					
E350 4matic (wagon)					
A-7, 3.5L, 6cyl	21	19/26	$2,700	5	P SS
E63 AMG 4matic (wagon)					
A-7, 5.5L, 8cyl	17	15/21	$3,350	3	P T SS
E63 AMG S 4matic (wagon)					
A-7, 5.5L, 8cyl	17	15/21	$3,350	3	P T SS
TOYOTA					
Prius v					
AV, 1.8L, 4cyl	**42**	**44/40**	**$1,250**	**9**	**HEV SS**

Manufacturer Model Configuration (trans, eng size, cyl)	MPG Comb	City/Hwy	Annual Fuel Cost	GHG Rating	Notes
SMALL PICKUP TRUCKS 2WD					
NISSAN					
Frontier 2WD					
A-5, 2.5L, 4cyl	19	17/23	$2,700	4	
M-5, 2.5L, 4cyl	21	19/23	$2,450	5	
A-5, 4.0L, 6cyl	18	16/22	$2,850	4	
M-6, 4.0L, 6cyl	19	16/22	$2,700	4	
TOYOTA					
Tacoma 2WD					
A-4, 2.7L, 4cyl	21	19/24	$2,450	5	
▶ M-5, 2.7L, 4cyl	23	21/25	$2,250	6	
A-5, 4.0L, 6cyl	19	17/21	$2,700	4	
M-6, 4.0L, 6cyl	18	16/21	$2,850	4	
SMALL PICKUP TRUCKS 4WD					
NISSAN					
Frontier 4WD					
A-5, 4.0L, 6cyl	17	15/21	$3,050	3	
M-6, 4.0L, 6cyl	18	16/21	$2,850	4	
TOYOTA					
Tacoma 4WD					
A-4, 2.7L, 4cyl	19	18/21	$2,700	4	PT4WD
M-5, 2.7L, 4cyl	19	18/21	$2,700	4	PT4WD
A-5, 4.0L, 6cyl	18	16/21	$2,850	4	PT4WD
M-6, 4.0L, 6cyl	17	16/19	$3,050	3	PT4WD
STANDARD PICKUP TRUCKS 2WD					
CHEVROLET					
Silverado C15 2WD					
A-6, 6.2L, 8cyl	17	15/21	$3,050	3	
A-6, 4.3L, 6cyl	20	18/24	$2,600	5	Gas
	14	12/16	$3,250	4	E85
A-6, 5.3L, 8cyl	19	16/23	$2,700	4	Gas
	14	12/17	$3,250	5	E85
FORD					
F150 Pickup 2WD					
A-S6, 3.5L, 6cyl	18	16/22	$2,850	4	T
A-6, 3.5L, 6cyl	18	16/22	$2,850	4	T
A-S6, 6.2L, 8cyl	15	13/18	$3,450	2	
F150 Pickup 2WD FFV					
A-S6, 3.7L, 6cyl	19	17/23	$2,700	4	Gas
	14	12/17	$3,250	5	E85
A-6, 3.7L, 6cyl	19	17/23	$2,700	4	Gas
	14	12/17	$3,250	5	E85
A-S6, 5.0L, 8cyl	17	15/21	$3,050	3	Gas
	13	11/15	$3,500	4	E85
A-6, 5.0L, 8cyl	17	15/21	$3,050	3	Gas
	13	11/15	$3,500	4	E85

Manufacturer Model Configuration (trans, eng size, cyl)	MPG Comb	City/Hwy	Annual Fuel Cost	GHG Rating	Notes
GMC					
Sierra C15 2WD					
A-6, 6.2L, 8cyl	17	15/21	$3,050	3	
A-6, 4.3L, 6cyl	20	18/24	$2,600	5	Gas
	14	12/16	$3,250	4	E85
A-6, 5.3L, 8cyl	19	16/23	$2,700	4	Gas
	14	12/17	$3,250	5	E85
NISSAN					
Titan 2WD					
A-5, 5.6L, 8cyl	15	13/18	$3,450	2	
A-5, 5.6L, 8cyl	15	13/18	$3,450	2	Gas
	11	9/13	$4,150	2	E85
RAM					
1500 2WD					
A-8, 3.6L, 6cyl	20	17/25	$2,600	5	
A-6, 5.7L, 8cyl	16	14/20	$3,400	3	Mid
A-8, 5.7L, 8cyl	17	15/22	$3,200	3	Mid
▶ A-8, 3.0L, 6cyl	23	20/28	$2,600	5	D T
A-8, 3.6L, 6cyl	20	17/25	$2,600	5	Gas
	14	12/17	$3,250	5	E85
1500 HFE 2WD					
A-8, 3.6L, 6cyl	21	18/25	$2,450	5	SS
ROUSH PERFORMANCE					
F150 Pickup 2WD					
A-S6, 5.0L, 8cyl	13	12/15	$4,350	1	P S
A-S6, 6.2L, 8cyl	11	10/12	$5,150	1	P S
TOYOTA					
Tundra 2WD					
A-S5, 4.0L, 6cyl	17	16/20	$3,050	3	
A-S6, 4.6L, 8cyl	16	15/19	$3,250	3	
A-S6, 5.7L, 8cyl	15	13/18	$3,450	2	
STANDARD PICKUP TRUCKS 4WD					
CHEVROLET					
Silverado K15 4WD					
A-6, 6.2L, 8cyl	17	14/20	$3,050	3	
A-6, 4.3L, 6cyl	19	17/22	$2,700	4	Gas
	13	12/15	$3,500	4	E85
A-6, 5.3L, 8cyl	18	16/22	$2,850	4	Gas
	13	12/16	$3,500	4	E85
FORD					
F150 Pickup 4WD					
A-S6, 3.5L, 6cyl	17	15/21	$3,050	3	T PT4WD
A-6, 3.5L, 6cyl	17	15/21	$3,050	3	T PT4WD
A-S6, 6.2L, 8cyl	13	12/16	$3,950	1	PT4WD

F150 Pickup 4WD FFV

Manufacturer Model Configuration (trans, eng size, cyl)	MPG Comb	MPG City/Hwy	Annual Fuel Cost	GHG Rating	Notes
A-S6, 3.7L, 6cyl	18	16/21	$2,850	4	Gas PT4WD
	13	11/15	$3,500	4	E85
A-6, 3.7L, 6cyl	18	16/21	$2,850	4	Gas PT4WD
	13	11/15	$3,500	4	E85
A-S6, 5.0L, 8cyl	16	14/19	$3,250	3	Gas PT4WD
	12	10/14	$3,800	3	E85
A-6, 5.0L, 8cyl	16	14/19	$3,250	3	Gas PT4WD
	12	10/14	$3,800	3	E85

F150 Raptor Pickup 4WD

A-S6, 6.2L, 8cyl	13	11/16	$3,950	1	PT4WD

GMC
Sierra K15 4WD

A-6, 6.2L, 8cyl	17	14/20	$3,050	3	
A-6, 4.3L, 6cyl	19	17/22	$2,700	4	Gas
	13	12/15	$3,500	4	E85
A-6, 5.3L, 8cyl	18	16/22	$2,850	4	Gas
	13	12/16	$3,500	4	E85

HONDA
Ridgeline Truck 4WD

A-5, 3.5L, 6cyl	17	15/21	$3,050	3	

NISSAN
Titan 4WD

A-5, 5.6L, 8cyl	14	12/17	$3,700	2	
A-5, 5.6L, 8cyl	14	12/17	$3,700	2	Gas
	10	9/12	$4,550	2	E85

RAM
1500 4WD

A-8, 3.6L, 6cyl	19	16/23	$2,700	4	
A-6, 5.7L, 8cyl	15	13/19	$3,600	2	Mid
A-8, 5.7L, 8cyl	17	15/21	$3,200	3	Mid
A-8, 3.0L, 6cyl	22	19/27	$2,750	4	D T
A-8, 3.6L, 6cyl	19	16/23	$2,700	4	Gas
	13	11/16	$3,500	4	E85

ROUSH PERFORMANCE
F150 Pickup 4WD

A-S6, 5.0L, 8cyl	13	12/15	$4,350	1	P S
A-S6, 6.2L, 8cyl	11	10/12	$5,150	1	P S PT4WD

F150 Raptor Pickup 4WD

A-S6, 6.2L, 8cyl	11	10/12	$5,150	1	P S PT4WD

TOYOTA
Tundra 4WD

A-S6, 4.6L, 8cyl	16	14/18	$3,250	3	PT4WD
A-S6, 5.7L, 8cyl	15	13/17	$3,450	2	PT4WD

Tundra 4WD FFV

A-S6, 5.7L, 8cyl	15	13/17	$3,450	2	Gas PT4WD
	11	9/12	$4,150	2	E85

VANS, CARGO TYPE

CHEVROLET
Express 1500 2WD Cargo

Manufacturer Model Configuration (trans, eng size, cyl)	MPG Comb	MPG City/Hwy	Annual Fuel Cost	GHG Rating	Notes
▶ A-4, 4.3L, 6cyl	16	14/19	$3,250	3	
A-4, 5.3L, 8cyl	15	13/18	$3,450	2	Gas
	11	10/13	$4,150	3	E85

Express 1500 2WD Conversion Cargo

A-4, 5.3L, 8cyl	14	13/17	$3,700	2	Gas
	11	10/13	$4,150	2	E85

Express 1500 AWD Cargo

A-4, 5.3L, 8cyl	14	13/17	$3,700	2	Gas
	11	10/12	$4,150	3	E85

Express 1500 AWD Conversion Cargo

A-4, 5.3L, 8cyl	14	13/17	$3,700	2	Gas SS
	10	9/12	$4,550	2	E85

Express 2500 2WD Conversion Cargo MDPV

A-6, 6.0L, 8cyl	12	10/15	$4,300	1	Gas
	9	7/11	$5,050	1	E85

FORD
E150 Van FFV

A-4, 4.6L, 8cyl	15	13/16	$3,450	2	Gas
	11	10/12	$4,150	2	E85
A-4, 5.4L, 8cyl	14	12/16	$3,700	2	Gas
	10	9/12	$4,550	2	E85

E250 Van FFV

A-4, 4.6L, 8cyl	15	13/16	$3,450	2	Gas
	11	10/12	$4,150	2	E85
A-4, 5.4L, 8cyl	14	12/16	$3,700	2	Gas
	10	9/12	$4,550	2	E85

E350 Van

A-5, 6.8L, 10cyl	12	10/14	$4,300	1	

E350 Van FFV

A-4, 5.4L, 8cyl	13	12/16	$3,950	1	Gas
	10	9/12	$4,550	2	E85

GMC
Savana 1500 AWD (cargo)

A-4, 5.3L, 8cyl	14	13/17	$3,700	2	Gas
	11	10/12	$4,150	3	E85

Savana 1500 AWD Conversion (cargo)

A-4, 5.3L, 8cyl	14	13/17	$3,700	2	Gas
	10	9/12	$4,550	2	E85

Savana 1500 2WD (cargo)

▶ A-4, 4.3L, 6cyl	16	14/19	$3,250	3	
A-4, 5.3L, 8cyl	15	13/18	$3,450	2	Gas
	11	10/13	$4,150	3	E85

Manufacturer Model Configuration (trans, eng size, cyl)	MPG Comb	City/Hwy	Annual Fuel Cost	GHG Rating	Notes
Savana 1500 2WD Conversion (cargo)					
A-4, 5.3L, 8cyl	14	13/17	$3,700	2	Gas SS
	11	10/13	$4,150	2	E85
Savana 2500 2WD Conversion (cargo) MDPV					
A-6, 6.0L, 8cyl	12	10/15	$4,300	1	Gas
	9	7/11	$5,050	1	E85

VANS, PASSENGER TYPE

CHEVROLET

Express 1500 2WD Passenger					
▶ A-4, 5.3L, 8cyl	14	13/17	$3,700	2	Gas
	11	10/13	$4,150	2	E85
Express 1500 AWD Passenger					
▶ A-4, 5.3L, 8cyl	14	13/17	$3,700	2	Gas SS
	10	9/12	$4,550	2	E85
Express 2500 2WD Passenger MDPV					
A-6, 4.8L, 8cyl	13	11/17	$3,950	1	SS
A-6, 6.0L, 8cyl	13	11/16	$3,950	1	Gas
	9	8/11	$5,050	1	E85
Express 3500 2WD Passenger MDPV					
A-6, 4.8L, 8cyl	13	11/17	$3,950	1	SS
A-6, 6.0L, 8cyl	12	11/16	$4,300	1	Gas
	9	8/11	$5,050	1	E85

FORD

E150 Wagon FFV					
▶ A-4, 4.6L, 8cyl	14	13/16	$3,700	2	Gas
	10	9/12	$4,550	2	E85
A-4, 5.4L, 8cyl	13	12/16	$3,950	1	Gas
	10	9/12	$4,550	1	E85
E350 Wagon					
A-5, 6.8L, 10cyl	11	10/13	$4,700	1	
E350 Wagon FFV					
A-4, 5.4L, 8cyl	13	11/15	$3,950	1	Gas
	10	9/11	$4,550	1	E85

GMC

Savana 1500 2WD (Passenger)					
▶ A-4, 5.3L, 8cyl	14	13/17	$3,700	2	Gas
	11	10/13	$4,150	2	E85
Savana 1500 AWD (Passenger)					
▶ A-4, 5.3L, 8cyl	14	13/17	$3,700	2	Gas
	10	9/12	$4,550	2	E85
Savana 2500 2WD (Passenger) MDPV					
A-6, 4.8L, 8cyl	13	11/17	$3,950	1	
A-6, 6.0L, 8cyl	13	11/16	$3,950	1	Gas
	9	8/11	$5,050	1	E85

Manufacturer Model Configuration (trans, eng size, cyl)	MPG Comb	City/Hwy	Annual Fuel Cost	GHG Rating	Notes
Savana 3500 2WD (Passenger) MDPV					
A-6, 4.8L, 8cyl	13	11/17	$3,950	1	
A-6, 6.0L, 8cyl	12	11/16	$4,300	1	Gas
	9	8/11	$5,050	1	E85

SPECIAL PURPOSE VEHICLES 2WD

CADILLAC

XTS Hearse					
A-S6, 3.6L, 6cyl	17	15/21	$3,050	3	Tax
XTS Limo					
A-S6, 3.6L, 6cyl	17	15/21	$3,050	3	Tax

FORD

Transit Connect Van 2WD					
▶ A-S6, 1.6L, 4cyl	25	22/30	$2,050	6	T
A-S6, 2.5L, 4cyl	24	21/29	$2,150	6	
Transit Connect Wagon FWD					
▶ A-S6, 1.6L, 4cyl	25	22/29	$2,050	6	T
A-S6, 2.5L, 4cyl	23	20/28	$2,250	6	
Transit Connect Wagon LWB FWD					
A-S6, 2.5L, 4cyl	23	20/28	$2,250	6	

LINCOLN

MKT Livery FWD					
A-S6, 2.0L, 4cyl	23	20/28	$2,250	6	T

NISSAN

NV200 Cargo Van					
AV, 2.0L, 4cyl	24	24/25	$2,150	6	

SPECIAL PURPOSE VEHICLES 4WD

LINCOLN

MKT Livery AWD					
A-6, 3.7L, 6cyl	19	17/24	$2,700	4	

MINIVANS 2WD

CHRYSLER

Town and Country					
A-6, 3.6L, 6cyl	20	17/25	$2,600	5	
A-6, 3.6L, 6cyl	20	17/25	$2,600	5	Gas
	14	12/18	$3,250	5	E85

DODGE

Grand Caravan					
A-6, 3.6L, 6cyl	20	17/25	$2,600	5	
A-6, 3.6L, 6cyl	20	17/25	$2,600	5	Gas
	14	12/18	$3,250	5	E85

HONDA

Odyssey					
A-6, 3.5L, 6cyl	22	19/28	$2,350	5	

KIA

Sedona					
A-6, 3.5L, 6cyl	20	17/24	$2,600	5	

Manufacturer Model Configuration (trans, eng size, cyl)	MPG Comb	MPG City/Hwy	Annual Fuel Cost	GHG Rating	Notes
MAZDA					
5					
▶ A-S5, 2.5L, 4cyl	24	22/28	$2,150	6	
▶ M-6, 2.5L, 4cyl	24	21/28	$2,150	6	
NISSAN					
Quest					
AV, 3.5L, 6cyl	21	19/25	$2,450	5	
RAM					
C/V					
A-6, 3.6L, 6cyl	21	18/26	$2,450	5	Gas
	15	13/18	$3,050	5	E85
TOYOTA					
Sienna 2WD					
A-S6, 3.5L, 6cyl	21	18/25	$2,450	5	
VOLKSWAGEN					
Routan					
A-6, 3.6L, 6cyl	20	17/25	$2,600	5	Gas
	14	12/18	$3,250	5	E85

MINIVANS 4WD

Manufacturer Model Configuration (trans, eng size, cyl)	MPG Comb	MPG City/Hwy	Annual Fuel Cost	GHG Rating	Notes
TOYOTA					
Sienna AWD					
A-S6, 3.5L, 6cyl	19	16/23	$2,700	4	

SMALL SPORT UTILITY VEHICLES 2WD

Manufacturer Model Configuration (trans, eng size, cyl)	MPG Comb	MPG City/Hwy	Annual Fuel Cost	GHG Rating	Notes
ACURA					
MDX 2WD					
A-S6, 3.5L, 6cyl	23	20/28	$2,450	6	P
RDX 2WD					
A-S6, 3.5L, 6cyl	23	20/28	$2,450	6	P
BUICK					
Encore					
A-S6, 1.4L, 4cyl	28	25/33	$1,850	7	T
CHEVROLET					
Captiva FWD					
A-6, 2.4L, 4cyl	23	20/28	$2,250	6	Gas
	18	15/22	$2,550	6	E85
A-6, 3.0L, 6cyl	19	17/24	$2,700	4	Gas
	14	12/17	$3,250	5	E85
Equinox FWD					
A-6, 2.4L, 4cyl	26	22/32	$2,000	7	
A-6, 3.6L, 6cyl	20	17/24	$2,600	5	
A-6, 2.4L, 4cyl	26	22/32	$2,000	7	Gas
	18	15/22	$2,550	6	E85
A-6, 3.6L, 6cyl	20	17/24	$2,600	5	Gas
	16	13/22	$2,850	6	E85

Manufacturer Model Configuration (trans, eng size, cyl)	MPG Comb	MPG City/Hwy	Annual Fuel Cost	GHG Rating	Notes
DODGE					
Journey FWD					
A-4, 2.4L, 4cyl	21	19/26	$2,450	5	
A-6, 3.6L, 6cyl	19	17/25	$2,700	4	Gas
	14	12/18	$3,250	5	E85
FORD					
Edge FWD					
A-6, 2.0L, 4cyl	24	21/30	$2,150	6	T
A-S6, 3.5L, 6cyl	22	19/27	$2,350	5	
A-S6, 3.7L, 6cyl	21	18/26	$2,450	5	
Escape FWD					
A-S6, 1.6L, 4cyl	26	23/32	$2,000	7	T
A-S6, 2.0L, 4cyl	25	22/30	$2,050	6	T
A-S6, 2.5L, 4cyl	25	22/31	$2,050	6	
GMC					
Terrain FWD					
A-6, 2.4L, 4cyl	26	22/32	$2,000	7	
A-6, 3.6L, 6cyl	20	17/24	$2,600	5	
A-6, 2.4L, 4cyl	26	22/32	$2,000	7	Gas
	18	15/22	$2,550	6	E85
A-6, 3.6L, 6cyl	20	17/24	$2,600	5	Gas
	16	13/22	$2,850	6	E85
HONDA					
CR-V 2WD					
A-5, 2.4L, 4cyl	26	23/31	$2,000	7	
Crosstour 2WD					
A-5, 2.4L, 4cyl	25	22/31	$2,050	6	
A-S6, 3.5L, 6cyl	23	20/30	$2,250	6	
Pilot 2WD					
A-5, 3.5L, 6cyl	21	18/25	$2,450	5	
HYUNDAI					
Santa Fe 2WD					
A-6, 3.3L, 6cyl	21	18/25	$2,450	5	
Santa Fe Sport 2WD					
A-6, 2.0L, 4cyl	22	19/27	$2,350	5	T
A-6, 2.4L, 4cyl	23	20/27	$2,250	6	
Tucson 2WD					
A-6, 2.0L, 4cyl	25	23/29	$2,050	6	
A-6, 2.4L, 4cyl	24	21/28	$2,150	6	
INFINITI					
QX60 FWD					
AV-S7, 3.5L, 6cyl	22	20/26	$2,600	5	P
QX70 RWD					
A-S7, 3.7L, 6cyl	19	17/24	$3,000	4	P
JEEP					
Cherokee FWD					
A-9, 2.4L, 4cyl	25	22/31	$2,050	6	
A-9, 3.2L, 6cyl	22	19/28	$2,350	5	
Compass FWD					
AV, 2.0L, 4cyl	24	22/27	$2,150	6	
A-6, 2.0L, 4cyl	24	21/28	$2,150	6	
M-5, 2.0L, 4cyl	26	23/30	$2,000	7	
A-6, 2.4L, 4cyl	24	21/28	$2,150	6	
M-5, 2.4L, 4cyl	25	23/28	$2,050	6	

Manufacturer Model Configuration (trans, eng size, cyl)	MPG Comb	MPG City/Hwy	Annual Fuel Cost	GHG Rating	Notes
Patriot FWD					
AV, 2.0L, 4cyl	24	22/27	$2,150	6	
A-6, 2.0L, 4cyl	24	21/28	$2,150	6	
M-5, 2.0L, 4cyl	26	23/30	$2,000	7	
A-6, 2.4L, 4cyl	24	21/28	$2,150	6	
M-5, 2.4L, 4cyl	25	23/28	$2,050	6	
KIA					
Sorento 2WD					
A-6, 2.4L, 4cyl	22	20/26	$2,350	5	
M-6, 2.4L, 4cyl	21	19/27	$2,450	5	
A-6, 3.3L, 6cyl	21	18/25	$2,450	5	
Sportage 2WD					
A-6, 2.0L, 4cyl	23	20/26	$2,250	6	T
A-6, 2.4L, 4cyl	24	21/28	$2,150	6	
LEXUS					
RX 350					
A-S6, 3.5L, 6cyl	21	18/25	$2,450	5	
RX 450h					
AV-S6, 3.5L, 6cyl	30	32/28	$1,900	8	P HEV SS
LINCOLN					
MKX FWD					
A-S6, 3.7L, 6cyl	21	18/26	$2,450	5	
MAZDA					
CX-5 2WD					
A-S6, 2.0L, 4cyl	29	26/32	$1,800	7	
M-6, 2.0L, 4cyl	29	26/35	$1,800	7	
A-S6, 2.5L, 4cyl	27	25/32	$1,900	7	
CX-9 2WD					
A-S6, 3.7L, 6cyl	19	17/24	$2,700	4	
MERCEDES-BENZ					
GLK350					
A-7, 3.5L, 6cyl	22	19/26	$2,600	5	P PZEV SS
A-7, 3.5L, 6cyl	21	19/25	$2,700	5	P SS
MITSUBISHI					
Outlander 2WD					
AV-S6, 2.4L, 4cyl	27	25/31	$1,900	7	
Outlander Sport 2WD					
AV-S6, 2.0L, 4cyl	27	24/31	$1,900	7	
M-5, 2.0L, 4cyl	26	24/30	$2,000	7	
NISSAN					
Murano FWD					
AV, 3.5L, 6cyl	20	18/24	$2,600	5	
Pathfinder 2WD					
AV, 3.5L, 6cyl	22	20/26	$2,350	5	
Rogue FWD					
AV, 2.5L, 4cyl	28	26/33	$1,850	7	
Rogue Select FWD					
AV, 2.5L, 4cyl	25	23/28	$2,050	6	
Xterra 2WD					
A-5, 4.0L, 6cyl	18	16/22	$2,850	4	
TOYOTA					
FJ Cruiser 2WD					
A-5, 4.0L, 6cyl	18	16/20	$2,850	4	
Highlander 2WD					
A-S6, 2.7L, 4cyl	22	20/25	$2,350	5	
A-S6, 3.5L, 6cyl	21	19/25	$2,450	5	
RAV4					
A-S6, 2.5L, 4cyl	26	24/31	$2,000	7	
RAV4 EV					
▶ AV	76	78/74	$800	10	EV
Venza					
A-S6, 2.7L, 4cyl	23	20/26	$2,250	6	
A-S6, 3.5L, 6cyl	22	19/26	$2,350	5	
VOLKSWAGEN					
Tiguan					
A-S6, 2.0L, 4cyl	23	21/26	$2,450	6	P T
M-6, 2.0L, 4cyl	21	18/26	$2,700	5	P T
VOLVO					
XC60 FWD					
A-S6, 3.2L, 6cyl	21	18/26	$2,450	5	
XC70 FWD					
A-S6, 3.2L, 6cyl	21	18/26	$2,450	5	

SMALL SPORT UTILITY VEHICLES 4WD

Manufacturer Model Configuration (trans, eng size, cyl)	MPG Comb	MPG City/Hwy	Annual Fuel Cost	GHG Rating	Notes
ACURA					
MDX 4WD					
A-S6, 3.5L, 6cyl	21	18/27	$2,700	5	P
RDX 4WD					
A-S6, 3.5L, 6cyl	22	19/27	$2,600	5	P
AUDI					
Q5					
A-S8, 3.0L, 6cyl	21	18/26	$2,700	5	P S
A-S8, 3.0L, 6cyl	27	24/31	$2,250	6	D T SS
A-S8, 2.0L, 4cyl	23	20/28	$2,450	6	Gas P T
	16	14/19	$2,850	6	E85
Q5 Hybrid					
A-S8, 2.0L, 4cyl	26	24/30	$2,200	7	P T HEV SS
SQ5					
A-S8, 3.0L, 6cyl	19	16/23	$3,000	4	P S
BMW					
X3 xDrive28i					
A-S8, 2.0L, 4cyl	24	21/28	$2,350	6	P T SS
X3 xDrive35i					
A-S8, 3.0L, 6cyl	21	19/26	$2,700	5	P T SS
BUICK					
Encore AWD					
A-S6, 1.4L, 4cyl	26	23/30	$2,000	7	T
CHEVROLET					
Captiva AWD					
A-6, 3.0L, 6cyl	18	16/22	$2,850	4	Gas
	13	11/16	$3,500	4	E85

Manufacturer Model Configuration (trans, eng size, cyl)	MPG		Annual Fuel Cost	GHG Rating	Notes
	Comb	City/Hwy			
Equinox AWD					
A-6, 2.4L, 4cyl	23	20/29	$2,250	6	
A-6, 3.6L, 6cyl	19	16/23	$2,700	4	
A-6, 2.4L, 4cyl	23	20/29	$2,250	6	Gas
	17	14/20	$2,700	6	E85
A-6, 3.6L, 6cyl	19	16/23	$2,700	4	Gas
	14	12/17	$3,250	5	E85
DODGE					
Journey AWD					
A-6, 3.6L, 6cyl	19	16/24	$2,700	4	
FORD					
Edge AWD					
A-S6, 3.5L, 6cyl	21	18/25	$2,450	5	
A-S6, 3.7L, 6cyl	19	17/23	$2,700	4	
Escape AWD					
A-S6, 1.6L, 4cyl	25	22/30	$2,050	6	T
A-S6, 2.0L, 4cyl	24	21/28	$2,150	6	T
GMC					
Terrain AWD					
A-6, 2.4L, 4cyl	23	20/29	$2,250	6	
A-6, 3.6L, 6cyl	19	16/23	$2,700	4	
A-6, 2.4L, 4cyl	23	20/29	$2,250	6	Gas
	17	14/20	$2,700	6	E85
A-6, 3.6L, 6cyl	19	16/23	$2,700	4	Gas
	14	12/17	$3,250	5	E85
HONDA					
CR-V 4WD					
A-5, 2.4L, 4cyl	25	22/30	$2,050	6	
Crosstour 4WD					
A-S6, 3.5L, 6cyl	22	19/28	$2,350	5	
Pilot 4WD					
A-5, 3.5L, 6cyl	20	17/24	$2,600	5	
HYUNDAI					
Santa Fe 4WD					
A-6, 3.3L, 6cyl	20	18/24	$2,600	5	
Santa Fe Sport 4WD					
A-6, 2.0L, 4cyl	21	18/24	$2,450	5	T
A-6, 2.4L, 4cyl	21	19/25	$2,450	5	
Tucson 4WD					
A-6, 2.0L, 4cyl	23	21/25	$2,250	6	
A-6, 2.4L, 4cyl	22	20/25	$2,350	5	
INFINITI					
QX60 AWD					
AV-S7, 3.5L, 6cyl	21	19/25	$2,700	5	P
QX70 AWD					
A-S7, 3.7L, 6cyl	18	16/22	$3,150	4	P
A-S7, 5.0L, 8cyl	16	14/20	$3,550	3	P
JEEP					
Cherokee 4WD					
A-9, 2.4L, 4cyl	24	21/28	$2,150	6	
A-9, 3.2L, 6cyl	22	19/27	$2,350	5	

Manufacturer Model Configuration (trans, eng size, cyl)	MPG		Annual Fuel Cost	GHG Rating	Notes
	Comb	City/Hwy			
Cherokee 4WD Active Drive II					
A-9, 2.4L, 4cyl	23	21/27	$2,250	6	
A-9, 3.2L, 6cyl	21	19/26	$2,450	5	
Cherokee Trailhawk 4WD					
A-9, 2.4L, 4cyl	22	19/25	$2,350	5	
A-9, 3.2L, 6cyl	20	18/25	$2,600	5	
Compass 4WD					
AV, 2.4L, 4cyl	21	20/23	$2,450	5	
A-6, 2.4L, 4cyl	23	21/27	$2,250	6	
M-5, 2.4L, 4cyl	25	23/28	$2,050	6	
Patriot 4WD					
AV, 2.4L, 4cyl	21	20/23	$2,450	5	
A-6, 2.4L, 4cyl	23	21/27	$2,250	6	
M-5, 2.4L, 4cyl	25	23/28	$2,050	6	
Wrangler 4WD					
A-5, 3.6L, 6cyl	18	17/21	$2,850	4	
M-6, 3.6L, 6cyl	18	17/21	$2,850	4	
Wrangler Unlimited 4WD					
A-5, 3.6L, 6cyl	18	16/20	$2,850	4	
M-6, 3.6L, 6cyl	18	16/21	$2,850	4	
KIA					
Sorento 4WD					
A-6, 2.4L, 4cyl	21	19/24	$2,450	5	
A-6, 3.3L, 6cyl	20	18/24	$2,600	5	
Sportage 4WD					
A-6, 2.0L, 4cyl	21	19/24	$2,450	5	T
A-6, 2.4L, 4cyl	22	19/26	$2,350	5	
LAND ROVER					
LR2					
A-S6, 2.0L, 4cyl	20	17/24	$2,850	5	P T
Range Rover Evoque					
A-S9, 2.0L, 4cyl	24	21/30	$2,350	6	P T
LEXUS					
RX 350 AWD					
A-S6, 3.5L, 6cyl	20	18/24	$2,600	5	
A-S8, 3.5L, 6cyl	21	18/26	$2,450	5	
RX 450h AWD					
AV-S6, 3.5L, 6cyl	29	30/28	$1,950	7	P HEV SS
LINCOLN					
MKT AWD					
A-S6, 3.5L, 6cyl	18	16/23	$2,850	4	T
MKX AWD					
A-S6, 3.7L, 6cyl	19	17/23	$2,700	4	
MAZDA					
CX-5 4WD					
A-S6, 2.0L, 4cyl	28	25/31	$1,850	7	
A-S6, 2.5L, 4cyl	26	24/30	$2,000	7	
CX-9 4WD					
A-S6, 3.7L, 6cyl	18	16/22	$2,850	4	
MERCEDES-BENZ					
GLK250 Bluetec 4matic					
A-7, 2.1L, 4cyl	28	24/33	$2,150	6	D T SS

Manufacturer Model Configuration (trans, eng size, cyl)	MPG Comb	City/Hwy	Annual Fuel Cost	GHG Rating	Notes
GLK350 4matic					
A-7, 3.5L, 6cyl	21	19/25	$2,700	5	P PZEV SS
A-7, 3.5L, 6cyl	21	18/25	$2,700	5	P SS
MITSUBISHI					
Outlander 4WD					
AV-S6, 2.4L, 4cyl	26	24/29	$2,000	7	
A-S6, 3.0L, 6cyl	23	20/28	$2,450	6	P
Outlander Sport 4WD					
AV-S6, 2.0L, 4cyl	26	24/29	$2,000	7	
NISSAN					
Murano AWD					
AV, 3.5L, 6cyl	20	18/23	$2,600	5	
Murano CrossCabriolet					
AV, 3.5L, 6cyl	19	17/22	$3,000	4	P
Pathfinder 4WD					
AV, 3.5L, 6cyl	21	19/25	$2,450	5	
Rogue AWD					
AV, 2.5L, 4cyl	28	25/32	$1,850	7	
Rogue Select AWD					
AV, 2.5L, 4cyl	24	22/27	$2,150	6	
Xterra 4WD					
A-5, 4.0L, 6cyl	17	15/20	$3,050	3	
M-6, 4.0L, 6cyl	17	16/20	$3,050	3	
SUBARU					
Forester AWD					
AV, 2.0L, 4cyl	25	23/28	$2,250	6	P T
AV, 2.5L, 4cyl	27	24/32	$1,900	7	
M-6, 2.5L, 4cyl	24	22/29	$2,150	6	
Outback AWD					
AV, 2.5L, 4cyl	26	24/30	$2,000	7	
M-6, 2.5L, 4cyl	24	22/29	$2,150	6	
A-S5, 3.6L, 6cyl	20	17/25	$2,600	5	
Tribeca AWD					
A-S5, 3.6L, 6cyl	18	16/21	$2,850	4	
XV Crosstrek AWD					
AV, 2.0L, 4cyl	28	25/33	$1,850	7	
M-5, 2.0L, 4cyl	26	23/30	$2,000	7	
XV Crosstrek Hybrid AWD					
▶ AV, 2.0L, 4cyl	31	29/33	$1,650	8	HEV SS
TOYOTA					
FJ Cruiser 4WD					
A-5, 4.0L, 6cyl	18	17/20	$2,850	4	PT4WD
M-6, 4.0L, 6cyl	16	15/18	$3,250	3	
RAV4 AWD					
A-S6, 2.5L, 4cyl	25	22/29	$2,050	6	
RAV4 Limited AWD					
A-S6, 2.5L, 4cyl	25	22/29	$2,050	6	
Venza 4WD					
A-S6, 2.7L, 4cyl	22	20/26	$2,350	5	
A-S6, 3.5L, 6cyl	21	18/25	$2,450	5	
VOLKSWAGEN					
Tiguan 4motion					
A-S6, 2.0L, 4cyl	23	20/26	$2,450	6	P T

Manufacturer Model Configuration (trans, eng size, cyl)	MPG Comb	City/Hwy	Annual Fuel Cost	GHG Rating	Notes
VOLVO					
XC60 AWD					
A-S6, 3.0L, 6cyl	20	17/24	$2,600	5	T
A-S6, 3.2L, 6cyl	20	18/25	$2,600	5	
XC70 AWD					
A-S6, 3.0L, 6cyl	20	17/24	$2,600	5	T
A-S6, 3.2L, 6cyl	21	18/25	$2,450	5	

STANDARD SPORT UTILITY VEHICLES 2WD

Manufacturer Model Configuration (trans, eng size, cyl)	MPG Comb	City/Hwy	Annual Fuel Cost	GHG Rating	Notes
BUICK					
Enclave FWD					
A-6, 3.6L, 6cyl	19	17/24	$2,700	4	
CADILLAC					
Escalade 2WD					
A-6, 6.2L, 8cyl	16	14/18	$3,250	3	Gas
	12	10/15	$3,800	3	E85
Escalade ESV 2WD					
A-6, 6.2L, 8cyl	16	14/18	$3,250	3	Gas
	12	10/15	$3,800	3	E85
SRX 2WD					
A-S6, 3.6L, 6cyl	19	17/24	$2,700	4	
CHEVROLET					
Suburban C10 2WD					
A-6, 5.3L, 8cyl	17	15/21	$3,050	3	Gas
	13	11/16	$3,500	4	E85
Tahoe C10 2WD					
A-6, 5.3L, 8cyl	17	15/21	$3,050	3	Gas
	13	11/16	$3,500	4	E85
Traverse FWD					
A-6, 3.6L, 6cyl	19	17/24	$2,700	4	
DODGE					
Durango RWD					
A-8, 5.7L, 8cyl	17	14/23	$3,200	3	Mid
A-8, 3.6L, 6cyl	20	18/25	$2,600	5	Gas
	15	13/19	$3,050	5	E85
FORD					
Expedition 2WD FFV					
A-6, 5.4L, 8cyl	16	14/20	$3,250	3	Gas
	12	10/14	$3,800	3	E85
Explorer 2WD FFV					
A-S6, 3.5L, 6cyl	20	17/24	$2,600	5	Gas
	15	13/18	$3,050	5	E85
Explorer FWD					
A-6, 2.0L, 4cyl	23	20/28	$2,250	6	T
A-S6, 3.5L, 6cyl	20	17/24	$2,600	5	
Flex FWD					
A-S6, 3.5L, 6cyl	20	18/25	$2,600	5	

GMC

Manufacturer Model Configuration (trans, eng size, cyl)	MPG Comb	MPG City/Hwy	Annual Fuel Cost	GHG Rating	Notes
Acadia FWD					
A-6, 3.6L, 6cyl	19	17/24	$2,700	4	
Yukon C10 2WD					
A-6, 5.3L, 8cyl	17	15/21	$3,050	3	Gas
	13	11/16	$3,500	4	E85
A-6, 6.2L, 8cyl	16	14/18	$3,250	3	Gas
	12	10/15	$3,800	3	E85
Yukon XL C10 2WD					
A-6, 5.3L, 8cyl	17	15/21	$3,050	3	Gas
	13	11/16	$3,500	4	E85
A-6, 6.2L, 8cyl	16	14/18	$3,250	3	Gas
	12	10/15	$3,800	3	E85

INFINITI

Manufacturer Model Configuration (trans, eng size, cyl)	MPG Comb	MPG City/Hwy	Annual Fuel Cost	GHG Rating	Notes
QX60 Hybrid FWD					
AV-S7, 2.5L, 4cyl	26	26/28	$2,000	7	S HEV SS
QX80 2WD					
A-S7, 5.6L, 8cyl	16	14/20	$3,550	3	P

JEEP

Manufacturer Model Configuration (trans, eng size, cyl)	MPG Comb	MPG City/Hwy	Annual Fuel Cost	GHG Rating	Notes
Grand Cherokee 2WD					
A-8, 5.7L, 8cyl	17	14/22	$3,200	3	Mid
A-8, 3.0L, 6cyl	25	22/30	$2,400	5	D T
A-8, 3.6L, 6cyl	20	17/25	$2,600	5	Gas
	16	14/19	$2,850	5	E85

LINCOLN

Manufacturer Model Configuration (trans, eng size, cyl)	MPG Comb	MPG City/Hwy	Annual Fuel Cost	GHG Rating	Notes
MKT FWD					
A-S6, 3.7L, 6cyl	20	17/25	$2,600	5	
Navigator 2WD FFV					
A-6, 5.4L, 8cyl	16	14/20	$3,250	3	Gas
	12	10/14	$3,800	3	E85

MERCEDES-BENZ

Manufacturer Model Configuration (trans, eng size, cyl)	MPG Comb	MPG City/Hwy	Annual Fuel Cost	GHG Rating	Notes
ML350					
A-7, 3.5L, 6cyl	20	18/24	$2,850	5	P

NISSAN

Manufacturer Model Configuration (trans, eng size, cyl)	MPG Comb	MPG City/Hwy	Annual Fuel Cost	GHG Rating	Notes
Armada 2WD					
A-5, 5.6L, 8cyl	15	13/19	$3,450	2	
A-5, 5.6L, 8cyl	15	12/19	$3,450	2	Gas
	11	9/13	$4,150	2	E85
Pathfinder Hybrid 2WD					
AV, 2.5L, 4cyl	26	25/28	$2,000	7	S HEV SS

TOYOTA

Manufacturer Model Configuration (trans, eng size, cyl)	MPG Comb	MPG City/Hwy	Annual Fuel Cost	GHG Rating	Notes
4Runner 2WD					
A-S5, 4.0L, 6cyl	19	17/22	$2,700	4	
Sequoia 2WD					
A-S6, 5.7L, 8cyl	15	13/17	$3,450	2	

VOLVO

Manufacturer Model Configuration (trans, eng size, cyl)	MPG Comb	MPG City/Hwy	Annual Fuel Cost	GHG Rating	Notes
XC90 FWD					
A-S6, 3.2L, 6cyl	19	16/25	$2,700	4	

STANDARD SPORT UTILITY VEHICLES 4WD

AUDI

Manufacturer Model Configuration (trans, eng size, cyl)	MPG Comb	MPG City/Hwy	Annual Fuel Cost	GHG Rating	Notes
Q7					
A-S8, 3.0L, 6cyl	18	16/22	$3,150	4	P S
A-S8, 3.0L, 6cyl	22	19/28	$2,750	4	D T

BMW

Manufacturer Model Configuration (trans, eng size, cyl)	MPG Comb	MPG City/Hwy	Annual Fuel Cost	GHG Rating	Notes
X5 sDrive35i					
A-S8, 3.0L, 6cyl	22	19/27	$2,600	5	P T SS
X5 xDrive35i					
A-S8, 3.0L, 6cyl	21	18/27	$2,700	5	P T SS
X5 xDrive50i					
A-S8, 4.4L, 8cyl	17	14/22	$3,350	3	P T SS
X6 M					
A-S6, 4.4L, 8cyl	15	13/17	$3,800	2	P T
X6 xDrive35i					
A-S8, 3.0L, 6cyl	20	17/24	$2,850	5	P T
X6 xDrive50i					
A-S8, 4.4L, 8cyl	17	14/21	$3,350	3	P T

BUICK

Manufacturer Model Configuration (trans, eng size, cyl)	MPG Comb	MPG City/Hwy	Annual Fuel Cost	GHG Rating	Notes
Enclave AWD					
A-6, 3.6L, 6cyl	18	16/22	$2,850	4	

CADILLAC

Manufacturer Model Configuration (trans, eng size, cyl)	MPG Comb	MPG City/Hwy	Annual Fuel Cost	GHG Rating	Notes
Escalade AWD					
A-6, 6.2L, 8cyl	15	13/18	$3,450	2	Gas
	12	10/14	$3,800	3	E85
Escalade ESV AWD					
A-6, 6.2L, 8cyl	14	13/18	$3,700	2	Gas
	10	9/13	$4,550	2	E85
SRX AWD					
A-S6, 3.6L, 6cyl	18	16/23	$2,850	4	

CHEVROLET

Manufacturer Model Configuration (trans, eng size, cyl)	MPG Comb	MPG City/Hwy	Annual Fuel Cost	GHG Rating	Notes
Suburban K10 4WD					
A-6, 5.3L, 8cyl	17	15/21	$3,050	3	Gas
	13	11/16	$3,500	4	E85
Tahoe K10 4WD					
A-6, 5.3L, 8cyl	17	15/21	$3,050	3	Gas
	13	11/16	$3,500	4	E85
Traverse AWD					
A-6, 3.6L, 6cyl	19	16/23	$2,700	4	

DODGE

Manufacturer Model Configuration (trans, eng size, cyl)	MPG Comb	MPG City/Hwy	Annual Fuel Cost	GHG Rating	Notes
Durango AWD					
A-8, 5.7L, 8cyl	16	14/22	$3,400	3	Mid
A-8, 3.6L, 6cyl	19	17/24	$2,700	4	Gas
	15	13/18	$3,050	5	E85

FORD

Manufacturer Model Configuration (trans, eng size, cyl)	MPG Comb	MPG City/Hwy	Annual Fuel Cost	GHG Rating	Notes
Expedition 4WD FFV					
A-6, 5.4L, 8cyl	15	13/18	$3,450	2	Gas PT4WD
	11	9/13	$4,150	2	E85

Manufacturer Model Configuration (trans, eng size, cyl)	MPG Comb	MPG City/Hwy	Annual Fuel Cost	GHG Rating	Notes
Explorer AWD					
A-S6, 3.5L, 6cyl	19	17/23	$2,700	4	
A-S6, 3.5L, 6cyl	18	16/22	$2,850	4	T
Explorer AWD FFV					
A-S6, 3.5L, 6cyl	19	17/23	$2,700	4	Gas
	14	12/17	$3,250	5	E85
Flex AWD					
A-S6, 3.5L, 6cyl	19	17/23	$2,700	4	
A-S6, 3.5L, 6cyl	18	16/23	$2,850	4	T
GMC					
Acadia AWD					
A-6, 3.6L, 6cyl	18	16/23	$2,850	4	
Yukon Denali K10 AWD					
A-6, 6.2L, 8cyl	15	13/18	$3,450	2	Gas
	12	10/14	$3,800	3	E85
Yukon K10 4WD					
A-6, 5.3L, 8cyl	17	15/21	$3,050	3	Gas
	13	11/16	$3,500	4	E85
Yukon XL K10 4WD					
A-6, 5.3L, 8cyl	17	15/21	$3,050	3	Gas
	13	11/16	$3,500	4	E85
Yukon XL K10 AWD					
A-6, 6.2L, 8cyl	14	13/18	$3,700	2	Gas
	10	9/13	$4,550	2	E85
INFINITI					
QX60 Hybrid AWD					
AV-S7, 2.5L, 4cyl	26	25/28	$2,000	7	S HEV SS
QX80 4WD					
A-S7, 5.6L, 8cyl	16	14/20	$3,550	3	P
JEEP					
Grand Cherokee 4WD					
A-8, 5.7L, 8cyl	16	14/20	$3,400	3	Mid
A-8, 3.0L, 6cyl	24	21/28	$2,500	5	D T
A-8, 3.6L, 6cyl	19	17/24	$2,700	4	Gas
	15	13/18	$3,050	5	E85
Grand Cherokee SRT8					
A-8, 6.4L, 8cyl	15	13/19	$3,800	2	P
LAND ROVER					
LR4					
A-S8, 3.0L, 6cyl	16	14/19	$3,550	3	P S SS
Range Rover					
A-S8, 3.0L, 6cyl	19	17/23	$3,000	4	P S SS
A-S8, 5.0L, 8cyl	15	13/19	$3,800	2	P S SS
Range Rover FFV					
A-S8, 3.0L, 6cyl	19	17/23	$3,000	4	Gas P S SS
	14	12/16	$3,250	4	E85
A-S8, 5.0L, 8cyl	16	14/19	$3,550	3	Gas P S SS
	11	9/14	$4,150	3	E85

Manufacturer Model Configuration (trans, eng size, cyl)	MPG Comb	MPG City/Hwy	Annual Fuel Cost	GHG Rating	Notes
Range Rover L FFV					
A-S8, 3.0L, 6cyl	19	17/23	$3,000	4	Gas P S SS
	14	12/16	$3,250	4	E85
A-S8, 5.0L, 8cyl	16	14/19	$3,550	3	Gas P S SS
	11	9/14	$4,150	3	E85
Range Rover Sport					
A-S8, 3.0L, 6cyl	19	17/23	$3,000	4	P S SS
A-S8, 5.0L, 8cyl	16	14/19	$3,550	3	P S SS
Range Rover Sport FFV					
A-S8, 3.0L, 6cyl	19	17/23	$3,000	4	Gas P S SS
	14	12/16	$3,250	4	E85
A-S8, 5.0L, 8cyl	16	14/19	$3,550	3	Gas P S SS
	11	10/14	$4,150	3	E85
LEXUS					
GX 460					
A-S6, 4.6L, 8cyl	17	15/20	$3,350	3	P
LX 570					
A-S6, 5.7L, 8cyl	14	12/17	$4,050	2	P
LINCOLN					
Navigator 4WD FFV					
A-6, 5.4L, 8cyl	15	13/18	$3,450	2	Gas PT4WD
	11	9/13	$4,150	2	E85
MERCEDES-BENZ					
G550					
A-7, 5.5L, 8cyl	13	12/15	$4,350	1	P
G63 AMG					
A-7, 5.5L, 8cyl	13	12/14	$4,350	1	P T
GL350 Bluetec 4matic					
A-7, 3.0L, 6cyl	22	19/26	$2,750	4	D T
GL450 4matic					
A-7, 4.7L, 8cyl	16	14/19	$3,550	3	P T
GL550 4matic					
A-7, 4.7L, 8cyl	15	13/18	$3,800	2	P T
GL63 AMG					
A-7, 5.5L, 8cyl	14	13/17	$4,050	2	P T
ML350 4matic					
A-7, 3.5L, 6cyl	19	17/22	$3,000	4	P
A-7, 3.5L, 6cyl	19	17/22	$3,000	4	Gas P
	15	13/17	$3,050	5	E85
ML350 Bluetec 4matic					
A-7, 3.0L, 6cyl	23	20/28	$2,600	5	D T
ML550 4matic					
A-7, 4.7L, 8cyl	16	14/19	$3,550	3	P T
ML63 AMG					
A-7, 5.5L, 8cyl	15	13/17	$3,800	2	P T

Manufacturer Model Configuration (trans, eng size, cyl)	MPG		Annual Fuel Cost	GHG Rating	Notes
	Comb	City/Hwy			

NISSAN

Armada 4WD
A-5, 5.6L, 8cyl	14	12/18	$3,700	2	
A-5, 5.6L, 8cyl	14	12/18	$3,700	2	Gas
	11	9/13	$4,150	2	E85

Pathfinder Hybrid 4WD
AV, 2.5L, 4cyl	26	25/27	$2,000	7	S HEV SS

PORSCHE

Cayenne
A-S8, 3.6L, 6cyl	20	17/23	$2,850	5	P SS
M-6, 3.6L, 6cyl	17	15/22	$3,350	3	P

Cayenne Diesel
A-S8, 3.0L, 6cyl	23	20/29	$2,600	5	D T

Cayenne GTS
A-8, 4.8L, 8cyl	17	15/21	$3,350	3	P

Cayenne S
A-8, 4.8L, 8cyl	18	16/22	$3,150	4	P

Cayenne S Hybrid
A-8, 3.0L, 6cyl	21	20/24	$2,700	5	P S HEV SS

Cayenne Turbo
A-8, 4.8L, 8cyl	17	15/22	$3,350	3	P T

Cayenne Turbo S
A-8, 4.8L, 8cyl	16	14/20	$3,550	3	P T SS

TOYOTA

4Runner 4WD
A-S5, 4.0L, 6cyl	18	17/21	$2,850	4	PT4WD
A-S5, 4.0L, 6cyl	18	17/21	$2,850	4	

Highlander AWD
A-S6, 3.5L, 6cyl	20	18/24	$2,600	5	

Highlander Hybrid 4WD
▶ AV-S6, 3.5L, 6cyl	28	27/28	$1,850	7	HEV SS

Highlander Hybrid 4WD LE Plus
▶ AV-S6, 3.5L, 6cyl	28	28/28	$1,850	7	HEV SS

Land Cruiser Wagon 4WD
A-S6, 5.7L, 8cyl	15	13/18	$3,450	2	

Sequoia 4WD
A-S6, 5.7L, 8cyl	14	13/17	$3,700	2	PT4WD

Sequoia 4WD FFV
A-S6, 5.7L, 8cyl	14	13/17	$3,700	2	Gas PT4WD
	10	9/12	$4,550	2	E85

VOLKSWAGEN

Touareg
A-S8, 3.6L, 6cyl	19	17/23	$3,000	4	P
A-S8, 3.0L, 6cyl	23	20/29	$2,600	5	D T

Touareg Hybrid
A-S8, 3.0L, 6cyl	21	20/24	$2,700	5	P S HEV SS

VOLVO

XC90 AWD
A-S6, 3.2L, 6cyl	18	16/23	$2,850	4	

DIESEL VEHICLES

Diesel-powered vehicles typically get 30-35% more miles per gallon than comparable vehicles powered by gasoline. Diesel engines are inherently more energy-efficient, and diesel fuel contains 10% more energy per gallon than gasoline. In addition, new advances in diesel engine technology have improved performance, reduced engine noise and fuel odor, and decreased emissions of harmful air pollutants. Ultra-low sulfur diesel fuels also help reduce emissions from these vehicles.

Annual fuel costs below are estimated assuming 15,000 miles of travel each year (55% city and 45% highway) and a diesel fuel cost of $4.02 per gallon.

Manufacturer Model Configuration (trans, eng size, cyl)	MPG		Annual Fuel Cost	GHG Rating	Notes
	Comb	City/Hwy			
SUBCOMPACT CARS					
VOLKSWAGEN					
Beetle Convertible					
AM-S6, 2.0L, 4cyl	31	28/37	$1,950	7	D T
M-6, 2.0L, 4cyl	32	28/41	$1,900	7	D T
COMPACT CARS					
BMW					
328d					
A-S8, 2.0L, 4cyl	37	32/45	$1,650	8	D T
328d xDrive					
A-S8, 2.0L, 4cyl	35	31/43	$1,750	8	D T
VOLKSWAGEN					
Beetle					
AM-S6, 2.0L, 4cyl	32	29/39	$1,900	7	D T
M-6, 2.0L, 4cyl	32	28/41	$1,900	7	D T
Golf					
AM-S6, 2.0L, 4cyl	34	30/42	$1,750	8	D T
M-6, 2.0L, 4cyl	34	30/42	$1,750	8	D T
Jetta					
AM-S6, 2.0L, 4cyl	34	30/42	$1,750	8	D T
M-6, 2.0L, 4cyl	34	30/42	$1,750	8	D T
MIDSIZE CARS					
AUDI					
A6 quattro					
A-S8, 3.0L, 6cyl	29	24/38	$2,100	7	D T SS
A7 quattro					
A-S8, 3.0L, 6cyl	29	24/38	$2,100	7	D T SS
BMW					
535d					
A-S8, 3.0L, 6cyl	30	26/38	$2,000	7	D T
535d xDrive					
A-S8, 3.0L, 6cyl	30	26/37	$2,000	7	D T
CHEVROLET					
Cruze					
A-S6, 2.0L, 4cyl	33	27/46	$1,850	7	D T
MERCEDES-BENZ					
E250 Bluetec					
A-7, 2.1L, 4cyl	34	28/45	$1,750	8	D T SS
E250 Bluetec 4matic					
A-7, 2.1L, 4cyl	32	27/42	$1,900	7	D T SS
VOLKSWAGEN					
Passat					
AM-S6, 2.0L, 4cyl	34	30/40	$1,750	8	D T
M-6, 2.0L, 4cyl	35	31/43	$1,750	8	D T

Manufacturer Model Configuration (trans, eng size, cyl)	MPG		Annual Fuel Cost	GHG Rating	Notes
	Comb	City/Hwy			
LARGE CARS					
AUDI					
A8 L					
A-S8, 3.0L, 6cyl	28	24/36	$2,150	6	D T SS
SMALL STATION WAGONS					
BMW					
328d xDrive Sports Wagon					
A-S8, 2.0L, 4cyl	35	31/43	$1,750	8	D T
VOLKSWAGEN					
Jetta SportWagen					
AM-S6, 2.0L, 4cyl	33	29/39	$1,850	7	D T
M-6, 2.0L, 4cyl	34	30/42	$1,750	8	D T
STANDARD PICKUP TRUCKS 2WD					
RAM					
1500 2WD					
A-8, 3.0L, 6cyl	23	20/28	$2,600	5	D T
STANDARD PICKUP TRUCKS 4WD					
RAM					
1500 4WD					
A-8, 3.0L, 6cyl	22	19/27	$2,750	4	D T
SMALL SPORT UTILITY VEHICLES 4WD					
AUDI					
Q5					
A-S8, 3.0L, 6cyl	27	24/31	$2,250	6	D T SS
MERCEDES-BENZ					
GLK250 Bluetec 4matic					
A-7, 2.1L, 4cyl	28	24/33	$2,150	6	D T SS
STANDARD SPORT UTILITY VEHICLES 2WD					
JEEP					
Grand Cherokee 2WD					
A-8, 3.0L, 6cyl	25	22/30	$2,400	5	D T

Manufacturer Model Configuration (trans, eng size, cyl)	MPG		Annual Fuel Cost	GHG Rating	Notes
	Comb	City/Hwy			

STANDARD SPORT UTILITY VEHICLES 4WD

AUDI
Q7
| A-S8, 3.0L, 6cyl | 22 | 19/28 | $2,750 | 4 | D T |

BMW
X5 xDrive35d
| A-S8, 3.0L, 6cyl | NA | NA | NA | NA | D |

JEEP
Grand Cherokee 4WD
| A-8, 3.0L, 6cyl | 24 | 21/28 | $2,500 | 5 | D T |

MERCEDES-BENZ
GL350 Bluetec 4matic
| A-7, 3.0L, 6cyl | 22 | 19/26 | $2,750 | 4 | D T |

ML350 Bluetec 4matic
| A-7, 3.0L, 6cyl | 23 | 20/28 | $2,600 | 5 | D T |

PORSCHE
Cayenne Diesel
| A-S8, 3.0L, 6cyl | 23 | 20/29 | $2,600 | 5 | D T |

VOLKSWAGEN
Touareg
| A-S8, 3.0L, 6cyl | 23 | 20/29 | $2,600 | 5 | D T |

COMPRESSED NATURAL GAS VEHICLES

Compressed natural gas (CNG) vehicles produce fewer smog-forming and greenhouse gas pollutants and reduce our dependence on petroleum. CNG fuel is normally dispensed in "equivalent gallons," where one gasoline gallon equivalent is equal to 121.5 standard cubit feet of natural gas.

	Transmission Type/Speeds	Engine Size/ Cylinders	MPGe Comb/City/Hwy	Annual Fuel cost	Driving Range (miles)
COMPACT CARS					
HONDA					
Civic Natural Gas	A-5	1.8L, 4cyl	31/27/38	$1,000	192

FUEL CELL VEHICLES

Fuel cell vehicles (FCVs) may not reach the mass market for a decade or more, but a limited number will be available for sale or lease in 2013-14 to demonstration fleets in areas with a readily accessible hydrogen supply. FCVs are propelled by electric motors powered by fuel cells, which produce electricity from the chemical energy of hydrogen. Fuel cell technology is more efficient than internal combustion engines and environmentally cleaner—the only by-product of a hydrogen fuel cell is water. However, several challenges must be overcome before FCVs are mass-marketed and sold at local dealerships. For more information about FCVs, visit **www.fueleconomy.gov** and the Fuel Cell Technologies Program website at **www.eere.energy.gov/hydrogenandfuelcells/**.

	Fuel Cell Type	Motor Type & Power	Battery Type & Rating	Fuel Type	Miles Per Kilogram Comb/City/Hwy	Driving Range (miles)
MIDSIZE CARS						
HONDA						
FCX Clarity	PEM*	100 kW AC Synchronous Permanent Magnet	288V Li-Ion	Hydogen	NA	NA

Note: The 2014 FCX Clarity will be available for lease to customers in Southern California—limited availability.

* Proton exchange membrane

ELECTRIC VEHICLES

Electric vehicles (EVs), also called "battery electric vehicles," are propelled by one or more electric motors powered by rechargeable battery packs. EVs are energy-efficient and reduce our dependence on petroleum since electricity is produced from domestic resources. They emit no tailpipe pollutants, although the power plant producing the electricity may emit pollution.

Electric motors have several performance benefits. They are quiet. have instant torque for quick acceleration, and require less maintenance than internal combustion engines.

Current EVs have a shorter driving range than gasoline or hybrid vehicles, and their range is more sensitive to driving style, driving conditions, and accessory use. Fully recharging the battery pack can take several hours—though a "quick charge" to 80% capacity may take as little as 30 minutes—and options for charging the vehicle away from home may be limited. EVs are also more expensive than comparable conventional vehicles and hybrids due to the cost of the large battery packs. Still, manufacturers are working hard to improve the driving range and reduce the cost of these vehicles, and public charging stations are becoming more common.

A federal income tax credit of up to $7,500 is currently available to consumers purchasing a qualifying EV. Visit **www.fueleconomy.gov** for additional information on EVs, including tax incentives.

Model	Motor	Battery Type	Fuel Economy (comb/city/hwy)		Range* (miles)	Charge Time (hrs @ 240V)	GHG Rating	Annual Fuel Cost
			MPGe	kWH/100 mi				
TWO SEATERS								
SMART								
fortwo electric drive convertible	55 kW DCPM†	Li-Ion	107/122/93	32/28/36	68	6	10	$600
fortwo electric drive coupe	55 kW DCPM†	Li-Ion	107/122/93	32/28/36	68	6	10	$600
MINICOMPACT CARS								
FIAT								
500e	82 kW ACIPM‡	Li-Ion	116/122/108	29/28/31	87	4	10	$500
SUBCOMPACT CARS								
BMW								
i3	125 kW Synchronous	Li-Ion	NA	NA	NA	NA	NA	NA
CHEVROLET								
Spark EV	104 kW AC Induction‡	Li-Ion	119/128/109	28/26/31	82	7	10	$500
COMPACT CARS								
FORD								
Focus Electric	107 kW AC PMSM§	Li-Ion	105/110/99	32/31/34	76	3.6	10	$600
MIDSIZE CARS								
NISSAN								
Leaf	80 kW DCPM†	Li-Ion	114/126/101	30/27/33	84	8	10	$550
LARGE CARS								
TESLA								
Model S (60 kWh battery pack)	225 kW AC Induction‡	Li-Ion	NA	NA	NA	NA	NA	NA
Model S (85 kWh battery pack)	270 kW AC Induction‡	Li-Ion	NA	NA	NA	NA	NA	NA
SMALL STATION WAGONS								
HONDA								
Fit EV	92 kW DCPM†	Li-Ion	118/132/105	29/26/32	82	4	10	$500
SMALL SPORT UTILITY VEHICLES 2WD								
TOYOTA								
RAV4 EV	115 kW AC Induction‡	Li-Ion	76/78/74	44/43/46	103	6	10	$800

* Range for combined city/highway driving (55% city and 45% highway)

† Direct current permanent magnet brushless motor

‡ Alternating current induction motor

§ Permanent magnet synchronous motor

PLUG-IN HYBRID ELECTRIC VEHICLES

Plug-in hybrid electric vehicles (PHEVs) are hybrids with high-capacity batteries that can be charged by plugging them into an electrical outlet or charging station. PHEVs can store enough electricity from the power grid to significantly reduce their petroleum consumption under typical driving conditions.

There are two basic PHEV configurations:

- **Series PHEVS, also called Extended Range Electric Vehicles (EREVs).** The electric motor of these vehicles is the only power scource thet turns the wheels; the gasoline engine only generates electricity. Series PHEVs can run solely on electricity until the battery needs to be recharged. The gasoline engine will then generate the electricity needed to power the electric motor. For short trips, these vehicles may not use any gasoline.

- **Parallel or Blended PHEVs.** Both the engine and electric motor are mechanically connected to the wheels, and both may propel the vehicle. The vehicle may operate using both electricity and gasoline at the same time, using electricity only, or using gasoline only.

PHEVs also have different battery capacities, allowing some to travel farther on electricity than others. PHEV fuel economy, like that of EVs and regular hybrids, can be sensitive to driving style, driving conditions, and accessory use. When operating in pure electric mode, PHEVs emit no tailpipe pollutants, although the power plant producing the electricity may emit pollution.

Charging a PHEV's battery typically takes several hours, but a "quick charge" to 80% capacity may take 30 minutes or less. However, PHEVs don't have to be plugged in to be driven. They can be fueled solely with gasoline, like a conventional hybrid, but they will not achieve maximum range or fuel economy without charging.

PHEVs use less petroleum and cost less to fuel than conventional hybrids, but they are more expensive to purchase.

A federal income tax credit of up to $7,500 is currently available to consumers purchasing a qualifying PHEV. Visit www.fueleconomy.gov for additional information on PHEVs, including tax incentives.

Manufacturer Model Eng. Size/No. Cyl, Elec. Motor	Fuel	Fuel Economy Combined MPGe — Comb / City / Hwy MPG	Range (miles)	Total Range* (miles)	Charge Time (hrs @ 240)	GHG Rating	Annual Fuel Cost
TWO SEATERS							
MCLAREN							
P1† 3.8L, 8cyl, 132 kW	NA	NA	NA	NA	NA	NA	NA
SUBCOMPACT CARS							
BMW							
i3 w Range Extender 0.6L, 2cyl, 125 kW Synchronous	NA	NA	NA	NA	NA	NA	NA
CADILLAC							
ELR 1.4L, 4cyl, 126 kW	Electricity / Premium Gasoline	82 MPGe ([41kWh 0 gal]/100 mi) / 33 / 31 / 35	37 / 307	340	5	10	$1050
COMPACT CARS							
CHEVROLET							
Volt 1.4L, 4cyl, 111 kW 3 phase AC	Electricity / Premium Gasoline	98 MPGe ([35kWh 0 gal]/100 mi) / 37 / 35 / 40	38 / 344	380	4	10	$900
MIDSIZE CARS							
FORD							
C-MAX Energi Plug-in Hybrid 2.0L, 4cyl, 68 kW DCPM‡	Electricity + Gasoline / Gasoline	100 MPGe ([34kWh 0 gal]/100 mi)§ / 43 / 44 / 41	21§ / 602	620	2.5	10	$950
Fusion Energi Plug-in Hybrid 2.0L, 4cyl, 68 kW DCPM‡	Electricity + Gasoline / Gasoline	100 MPGe ([34kWh 0 gal]/100 mi)§ / 43 / 44 / 41	21§ / 602	620	2.5	10	$950
HONDA							
Accord Plug-in Hybrid 2.0L, 4cyl, 124 kW DCPM‡	Electricity + Gasoline / Gasoline	115 MPGe ([29kWh 0 gal]/100 mi) / 46 / 47 / 46	13** / 561	570	0.67	10	$900
PORSCHE							
Panamera S E-Hybrid 3.0L, 6cyl, 71 kW	NA	NA	NA	NA	NA	NA	NA
TOYOTA							
Prius Plug-in Hybrid 1.8L, 4cyl, 18 kW AC	Electricity + Gasoline / Gasoline	95 MPGe ([29kWh 0.2 gal]/100 mi) / 50 / 51 / 49	11 / 530	540	1.5	10	$900

*   Total range is rounded to the nearest 10 miles.

†   Only available in selected areas of the U.S.

‡   Direct current permanent magnet brushless motor.

§   This vehicle did not use any gasoline for the first 21 miles in EPA tests. However, depending on how you drive the vehicle, you may use both gasoline and electricity during the fi rst 21 miles following a full charge.

** This vehicle did not use any gasoline for the first 13 miles in EPA tests. However, depending on how you drive the vehicle, you may use both gasoline and electricity during the first 13 miles following a full charge.

HYBRID-ELECTRIC VEHICLES

It's no coincidence that some of the most fuel-efficient vehicles for the 2014 model year are hybrid-electric vehicles (HEVs). Hybrids combine the best features of the internal combustion engine with an electric motor and can significantly improve fuel economy without sacrificing performance or driving range. HEVs may also be configured to provide increased performance rather than fuel economy.

HEVs are primarily propelled by an internal combustion engine, just like conventional vehicles. However, they also convert energy normally wasted during coasting and braking into electricity, which is stored in a battery until needed by the electric motor. The electric motor assists the engine when accelerating or hill climbing and at low speeds where internal combustion engines are least efficient. Unlike all-electric vehicles, HEVs do not need to be plugged into an external source of electricity to be recharged; conventional gasoline and regenerative braking provide all the energy the vehicle needs.

Annual fuel cost is estimated assuming 15,000 miles of travel each year (55% city and 45% highway) and a fuel cost of $3.44 per gallon for regular unleaded gasoline or $3.78 for premium gasoline.

Manufacturer Model Configuration (trans, eng size, cyl)	MPG		Annual Fuel Cost	GHG Rating	Battery Type
	Comb	City/Hwy			
TWO SEATERS					
HONDA					
CR-Z					
AV-S7, 1.5L, 4cyl	37	36/39	$1,400	9	144V Li-Ion
M-6, 1.5L, 4cyl	34	31/38	$1,500	8	144V Li-Ion
COMPACT CARS					
ACURA					
ILX Hybrid					
AV-S7, 1.5L, 4cyl	38	39/38	$1,500	9	144V Li-Ion
BMW					
ActiveHybrid 3					
A-S8, 3.0L, 6cyl	28	25/33	$2,000	7	374V Li-Ion
HONDA					
Civic Hybrid					
AV, 1.5L, 4cyl	45	44/47	$1,150	10	144V Li-Ion
Insight					
AV-S7, 1.3L, 4cyl	42	41/44	$1,250	9	101V Ni-MH
AV, 1.3L, 4cyl	42	41/44	$1,250	9	101V Ni-MH
INFINITI					
Q50 Hybrid					
A-S7, 3.5L, 6cyl	31	29/36	$1,850	8	346V Li-Ion
Q50 Hybrid AWD					
A-S7, 3.5L, 6cyl	30	28/35	$1,900	8	346V Li-Ion
Q50S Hybrid					
A-S7, 3.5L, 6cyl	30	28/34	$1,900	8	346V Li-Ion
Q50S Hybrid AWD					
A-S7, 3.5L, 6cyl	28	27/31	$2,000	7	346V Li-Ion
LEXUS					
CT 200h					
AV, 1.8L, 4cyl	42	43/40	$1,250	9	202V Ni-MH
TOYOTA					
Prius c					
AV, 1.5L, 4cyl	50	53/46	$1,050	10	144V Ni-MH
VOLKSWAGEN					
Jetta Hybrid					
AM-S7, 1.4L, 4cyl	45	42/48	$1,250	10	220V Li-Ion

Manufacturer Model Configuration (trans, eng size, cyl)	MPG		Annual Fuel Cost	GHG Rating	Battery Type
	Comb	City/Hwy			
MIDSIZE CARS					
ACURA					
RLX Hybrid					
A-S7, 3.5L, 6cyl	30	28/32	$1,900	8	260V Li-Ion
BMW					
ActiveHybrid 5					
A-S8, 3.0L, 6cyl	26	23/30	$2,200	7	374V Li-Ion
BUICK					
LaCrosse eAssist					
A-S6, 2.4L, 4cyl	29	25/36	$1,800	7	115V Li-Ion
Regal eAssist					
A-S6, 2.4L, 4cyl	29	25/36	$1,800	7	115V Li-Ion
CHEVROLET					
Malibu eAssist					
A-S6, 2.4L, 4cyl	29	25/36	$1,800	7	115V Li-Ion
FORD					
Fusion Hybrid FWD					
AV, 2.0L, 4cyl	47	47/47	$1,100	10	280V Li-Ion
HONDA					
Accord Hybrid					
AV, 2.0L, 4cyl	47	50/45	$1,100	10	259V Li-Ion
HYUNDAI					
Sonata Hybrid					
AM-6, 2.4L, 4cyl	38	36/40	$1,350	9	270V Li-Ion
Sonata Hybrid Limited					
AM-6, 2.4L, 4cyl	37	36/40	$1,400	9	270V Li-Ion
INFINITI					
Q70 Hybrid					
A-S7, 3.5L, 6cyl	31	29/34	$1,850	8	346V Li-Ion
KIA					
Optima Hybrid					
AM-6, 2.4L, 4cyl	38	36/40	$1,350	9	270V Li-Ion
Optima Hybrid EX					
AM-6, 2.4L, 4cyl	37	35/39	$1,400	9	270V Li-Ion
LEXUS					
ES 300h					
AV-S6, 2.5L, 4cyl	40	40/39	$1,300	9	245V Ni-MH
GS 450h					
AV-S8, 3.5L, 6cyl	31	29/34	$1,850	8	288V Ni-MH
LS 600h L					
AV-S8, 5.0L, 8cyl	20	19/23	$2,850	5	288V Ni-MH

Manufacturer Model Configuration (trans, eng size, cyl)	MPG		Annual Fuel Cost	GHG Rating	Battery Type
	Comb	City/Hwy			
LINCOLN					
MKZ Hybrid FWD AV, 2.0L, 4cyl	45	45/45	$1,150	10	280V Li-Ion
MERCEDES-BENZ					
E400 Hybrid A-7, 3.5L, 6cyl	26	24/30	$2,200	7	126V Li-Ion
TOYOTA					
Avalon Hybrid AV-S6, 2.5L, 4cyl	40	40/39	$1,300	9	245V Ni-MH
Camry Hybrid LE AV, 2.5L, 4cyl	41	43/39	$1,250	9	245V Ni-MH
Camry Hybrid XLE/SE AV, 2.5L, 4cyl	40	40/38	$1,300	9	245V Ni-MH
Prius AV, 1.8L, 4cyl	50	51/48	$1,050	10	202V Ni-MH

LARGE CARS

	Comb	City/Hwy	Annual Fuel Cost	GHG Rating	Battery Type
BMW					
ActiveHybrid 7L A-S8, 3.0L, 6cyl	25	22/30	$2,250	6	374V Li-Ion
CHEVROLET					
Impala eAssist A-S6, 2.4L, 4cyl	29	25/35	$1,800	7	115V Li-Ion
FORD					
C-MAX Hybrid FWD AV, 2.0L, 4cyl	43	45/40	$1,200	10	280V Li-Ion

MIDSIZE STATION WAGONS

	Comb	City/Hwy	Annual Fuel Cost	GHG Rating	Battery Type
TOYOTA					
Prius v AV, 1.8L, 4cyl	42	44/40	$1,250	9	202V Ni-MH

SMALL SPORT UTILITY VEHICLES 2WD

	Comb	City/Hwy	Annual Fuel Cost	GHG Rating	Battery Type
LEXUS					
RX 450h AV-S6, 3.5L, 6cyl	30	32/28	$1,900	8	288V Ni-MH

SMALL SPORT UTILITY VEHICLES 4WD

Manufacturer Model Configuration (trans, eng size, cyl)	MPG		Annual Fuel Cost	GHG Rating	Battery Type
	Comb	City/Hwy			
AUDI					
Q5 Hybrid A-S8, 2.0L, 4cyl	26	24/30	$2,200	7	266V Li-Ion
LEXUS					
RX 450h AWD AV-S6, 3.5L, 6cyl	29	30/28	$1,950	7	288V Ni-MH
SUBARU					
XV Crosstrek Hybrid AWD AV, 2.0L, 4cyl	31	29/33	$1,650	8	101V Ni-MH

STANDARD SPORT UTILITY VEHICLES 2WD

	Comb	City/Hwy	Annual Fuel Cost	GHG Rating	Battery Type
INFINITI					
QX60 Hybrid FWD AV-S7, 2.5L, 4cyl	26	26/28	$2,000	7	144V Li-Ion
NISSAN					
Pathfinder Hybrid 2WD AV, 2.5L, 4cyl	26	25/28	$2,000	7	144V Li-Ion

STANDARD SPORT UTILITY VEHICLES 4WD

	Comb	City/Hwy	Annual Fuel Cost	GHG Rating	Battery Type
INFINITI					
QX60 Hybrid AWD AV-S7, 2.5L, 4cyl	26	25/28	$2,000	7	144V Li-Ion
NISSAN					
Pathfinder Hybrid 4WD AV, 2.5L, 4cyl	26	25/27	$2,000	7	144V Li-Ion
PORSCHE					
Cayenne S Hybrid A-8, 3.0L, 6cyl	21	20/24	$2,700	5	288V Ni-MH
TOYOTA					
Highlander Hybrid 4WD AV-S6, 3.5L, 6cyl	28	27/28	$1,850	7	288V Ni-MH
Highlander Hybrid 4WD LE Plus AV-S6, 3.5L, 6cyl	28	28/28	$1,850	7	288V Ni-MH
VOLKSWAGEN					
Touareg Hybrid A-S8, 3.0L, 6cyl	21	20/24	$2,700	5	288V Ni-MH

ETHANOL FLEXIBLE FUEL VEHICLES

Ethanol flexible fuel vehicles (FFVs) are designed by the original manufacturer to operate on gasoline, E85, or any mixture of the two fuels. Annual fuel cost is estimated assuming 15,000 miles of travel each year (55% city and 45% highway) and an average fuel cost of $3.04 per gallon for E85, $3.44 per gallon for regular unleaded gasoline, and $3.78 per gallon for premium unleaded gasoline. The price of ethanol is highly variable from region to region; it is typically lower in the Midwestern United States and higher in other areas. Therefore, actual consumer experience may differ significantly from the annual fuel cost estimate presented here.

Fuel economy and driving range values are shown for both gasoline and E85. When operating your FFV on mixtures of gasoline and E85, such as when alternating between using these fuels, your driving range and fuel economy values will be somewhere between those listed for the two fuels, depending on the actual percentage of gasoline and E85 in the tank.

Manufacturer Model Configuration (trans, eng size, cyl)	MPG		Annual Fuel Cost	GHG Rating	Fuel	Range (miles)
	Comb	City/Hwy				
SUBCOMPACT CARS						
AUDI						
A5 Cabriolet quattro						
A-S8, 2.0L, 4cyl	24	20/29	$2,350	6	P	406
	16	14/20	$2,850	6	E85	270
A5 quattro						
A-S8, 2.0L, 4cyl	24	20/29	$2,350	6	P	406
	16	14/20	$2,850	6	E85	270
BENTLEY						
Continental GT Speed Convertible						
A-S8, 6.0L, 12cyl	15	12/20	$3,800	2	P	357
	11	9/15	$4,150	2	E85	262
Continental GTC						
A-S8, 6.0L, 12cyl	15	12/20	$3,800	2	P	357
	11	9/15	$4,150	2	E85	262
MERCEDES-BENZ						
E350 4matic Coupe						
A-7, 3.5L, 6cyl	23	20/28	$2,450	6	P	400
	17	15/21	$2,700	6	E85	300
E350 Convertible						
A-7, 3.5L, 6cyl	23	20/28	$2,450	6	P	400
	17	14/21	$2,700	6	E85	300
E350 Coupe						
A-7, 3.5L, 6cyl	23	20/29	$2,450	6	P	400
	18	15/22	$2,550	6	E85	310
COMPACT CARS						
AUDI						
A4 quattro						
A-S8, 2.0L, 4cyl	24	20/29	$2,350	6	P	406
	16	14/20	$2,850	6	E85	270
BENTLEY						
Continental GT						
A-S8, 6.0L, 12cyl	15	12/21	$3,800	2	P	357
	11	9/15	$4,150	2	E85	262
CHRYSLER						
200 Convertible						
A-6, 3.6L, 6cyl	22	19/29	$2,350	5	Gas	370
	16	14/21	$2,850	6	E85	275

Manufacturer Model Configuration (trans, eng size, cyl)	MPG		Annual Fuel Cost	GHG Rating	Fuel	Range (miles)
	Comb	City/Hwy				
FORD						
Focus FWD FFV						
AM-6, 2.0L, 4cyl	30	26/37	$1,700	8	Gas	372
	23	20/28	$2,000	8	E85	285
A-S6, 2.0L, 4cyl	30	26/37	$1,700	8	Gas	372
	23	20/28	$2,000	8	E85	285
M-5, 2.0L, 4cyl	30	26/36	$1,700	8	Gas	372
	22	19/26	$2,100	8	E85	273
Focus SFE FWD FFV						
AM-6, 2.0L, 4cyl	33	28/40	$1,550	8	Gas	409
	23	20/28	$2,000	8	E85	285
MERCEDES-BENZ						
C300 4matic						
A-7, 3.5L, 6cyl	22	20/27	$2,600	5	P	380
	16	14/20	$2,850	6	E85	280
C350						
A-7, 3.5L, 6cyl	23	20/29	$2,450	6	P	400
	17	15/21	$2,700	6	E85	300
MIDSIZE CARS						
BENTLEY						
Flying Spur						
A-S8, 6.0L, 12cyl	15	12/20	$3,800	2	P	357
	11	9/15	$4,150	2	E85	262
BUICK						
LaCrosse						
A-S6, 3.6L, 6cyl	21	18/28	$2,450	5	Gas	390
	16	14/20	$2,850	6	E85	300
LaCrosse AWD						
A-S6, 3.6L, 6cyl	20	17/26	$2,600	5	Gas	390
	14	12/18	$3,250	5	E85	270
CHRYSLER						
200						
A-6, 3.6L, 6cyl	22	19/29	$2,350	5	Gas	370
	16	14/21	$2,850	6	E85	275
DODGE						
Avenger						
A-6, 3.6L, 6cyl	22	19/29	$2,350	5	Gas	370
	16	14/21	$2,850	6	E85	275
Dart						
A-6, 2.0L, 4cyl	27	24/34	$1,900	7	Gas	383
	19	17/24	$2,400	7	E85	270

Manufacturer Model Configuration (trans, eng size, cyl)	MPG Comb	City/Hwy	Annual Fuel Cost	GHG Rating	Fuel	Range (miles)
JAGUAR						
XF FFV						
A-S8, 3.0L, 6cyl	21	17/28	$2,700	5	P	378
	15	13/19	$3,050	5	E85	270
A-S8, 5.0L, 8cyl	18	15/23	$3,150	4	P	324
	13	11/17	$3,500	4	E85	234
MERCEDES-BENZ						
E350						
A-7, 3.5L, 6cyl	24	21/31	$2,350	6	P	510
	18	16/23	$2,550	6	E85	380
E350 4matic						
A-7, 3.5L, 6cyl	24	20/29	$2,350	6	P	510
	17	15/21	$2,700	6	E85	360

LARGE CARS

Manufacturer Model Configuration (trans, eng size, cyl)	MPG Comb	City/Hwy	Annual Fuel Cost	GHG Rating	Fuel	Range (miles)
CHEVROLET						
Impala						
A-S6, 3.6L, 6cyl	22	19/29	$2,350	5	Gas	410
	16	14/20	$2,850	6	E85	300
Impala Limited						
A-6, 3.6L, 6cyl	22	18/30	$2,350	5	Gas	390
	16	13/22	$2,850	6	E85	280
CHRYSLER						
300						
A-8, 3.6L, 6cyl	23	19/31	$2,250	6	Gas	439
	17	14/23	$2,700	6	E85	325
300 AWD						
A-8, 3.6L, 6cyl	21	18/27	$2,450	5	Gas	401
	16	14/20	$2,850	6	E85	306
DODGE						
Charger						
A-5, 3.6L, 6cyl	21	18/27	$2,450	5	Gas	401
	15	13/19	$3,050	5	E85	287
A-8, 3.6L, 6cyl	23	19/31	$2,250	6	Gas	439
	17	14/23	$2,700	6	E85	325
Charger AWD						
A-8, 3.6L, 6cyl	21	18/27	$2,450	5	Gas	401
	16	14/20	$2,850	6	E85	306
FORD						
Taurus AWD FFV						
A-S6, 3.5L, 6cyl	21	18/26	$2,450	5	Gas	399
	15	13/19	$3,050	5	E85	285
Taurus FWD FFV						
A-S6, 3.5L, 6cyl	23	19/29	$2,250	6	Gas	437
	16	13/21	$2,850	6	E85	304
JAGUAR						
XJ FFV						
A-S8, 3.0L, 6cyl	21	18/27	$2,700	5	P	443
	14	12/19	$3,250	5	E85	295
A-S8, 5.0L, 8cyl	18	15/23	$3,150	4	P	380
	13	11/17	$3,500	4	E85	274
XJL FFV						
A-S8, 3.0L, 6cyl	20	17/27	$2,850	5	P	443
	14	11/19	$3,250	5	E85	295
A-S8, 5.0L, 8cyl	18	15/23	$3,150	4	P	380
	13	11/17	$3,500	4	E85	274

SMALL STATION WAGONS

Manufacturer Model Configuration (trans, eng size, cyl)	MPG Comb	City/Hwy	Annual Fuel Cost	GHG Rating	Fuel	Range (miles)
AUDI						
allroad quattro						
A-S8, 2.0L, 4cyl	23	20/27	$2,450	6	P	389
	15	14/18	$3,050	5	E85	254

STANDARD PICKUP TRUCKS 2WD

Manufacturer Model Configuration (trans, eng size, cyl)	MPG Comb	City/Hwy	Annual Fuel Cost	GHG Rating	Fuel	Range (miles)
CHEVROLET						
Silverado C15 2WD						
A-6, 4.3L, 6cyl	20	18/24	$2,600	5	Gas	520/680
	14	12/16	$3,250	4	E85	360/480
A-6, 5.3L, 8cyl	19	16/23	$2,700	4	Gas	490/650
	14	12/17	$3,250	5	E85	360/480
A-6, 6.2L, 8cyl	NA	NA	NA	NA	Gas	NA
	NA	NA	NA	NA	E85	NA
FORD						
F150 Pickup 2WD FFV						
A-S6, 3.7L, 6cyl	19	17/23	$2,700	4	Gas	494/684
	14	12/17	$3,250	5	E85	364/504
A-6, 3.7L, 6cyl	19	17/23	$2,700	4	Gas	494/684
	14	12/17	$3,250	5	E85	364/504
A-S6, 5.0L, 8cyl	17	15/21	$3,050	3	Gas	442/612
	13	11/15	$3,500	4	E85	338/468
A-6, 5.0L, 8cyl	17	15/21	$3,050	3	Gas	442/612
	13	11/15	$3,500	4	E85	338/468
GMC						
Sierra C15 2WD						
A-6, 4.3L, 6cyl	20	18/24	$2,600	5	Gas	520/680
	14	12/16	$3,250	4	E85	360/480
A-6, 5.3L, 8cyl	19	16/23	$2,700	4	Gas	490/650
	14	12/17	$3,250	5	E85	360/480
A-6, 6.2L, 8cyl	NA	NA	NA	NA	Gas	NA
	NA	NA	NA	NA	E85	NA
NISSAN						
Titan 2WD						
A-5, 5.6L, 8cyl	15	13/18	$3,450	2	Gas	420
	11	9/13	$4,150	2	E85	310
RAM						
1500 2WD						
A-8, 3.6L, 6cyl	20	17/25	$2,600	5	Gas	520/640
	14	12/17	$3,250	5	E85	364/448

STANDARD PICKUP TRUCKS 4WD

Manufacturer Model Configuration (trans, eng size, cyl)	MPG Comb	City/Hwy	Annual Fuel Cost	GHG Rating	Fuel	Range (miles)
CHEVROLET						
Silverado K15 4WD						
A-6, 4.3L, 6cyl	19	17/22	$2,700	4	Gas	490/650
	13	12/15	$3,500	4	E85	340/440
A-6, 5.3L, 8cyl	18	16/22	$2,850	4	Gas	470/610
	13	12/16	$3,500	4	E85	340/440
A-6, 6.2L, 8cyl	NA	NA	NA	NA	Gas	NA
	NA	NA	NA	NA	E85	NA

Manufacturer Model Configuration (trans, eng size, cyl)	MPG		Annual Fuel Cost	GHG Rating	Fuel	Range (miles)
	Comb	City/Hwy				

FORD

F150 Pickup 4WD FFV

A-S6, 3.7L, 6cyl	18	16/21	$2,850	4	Gas	468/648
	13	11/15	$3,500	4	E85	338/468
A-6, 3.7L, 6cyl	18	16/21	$2,850	4	Gas	468/648
	13	11/15	$3,500	4	E85	338/468
A-S6, 5.0L, 8cyl	16	14/19	$3,250	3	Gas	416/576
	12	10/14	$3,800	3	E85	312/432
A-6, 5.0L, 8cyl	16	14/19	$3,250	3	Gas	416/576
	12	10/14	$3,800	3	E85	312/432

GMC

Sierra K15 4WD

A-6, 4.3L, 6cyl	19	17/22	$2,700	4	Gas	490/650
	13	12/15	$3,500	4	E85	340/440
A-6, 5.3L, 8cyl	18	16/22	$2,850	4	Gas	470/610
	13	12/16	$3,500	4	E85	340/440
A-6, 6.2L, 8cyl	NA	NA	NA	NA	Gas	NA
	NA	NA	NA	NA	E85	NA

NISSAN

Titan 4WD

A-5, 5.6L, 8cyl	14	12/17	$3,700	2	Gas	390
	10	9/12	$4,550	2	E85	280

RAM

1500 4WD

A-8, 3.6L, 6cyl	19	16/23	$2,700	4	Gas	494/608
	13	11/16	$3,500	4	E85	338/416

TOYOTA

Tundra 4WD FFV

A-S6, 5.7L, 8cyl	15	13/17	$3,450	2	Gas	396
	11	9/12	$4,150	2	E85	290

VANS, CARGO TYPE

CHEVROLET

Express 1500 2WD Cargo

A-4, 5.3L, 8cyl	15	13/18	$3,450	2	Gas	470
	11	10/13	$4,150	3	E85	340

Express 1500 2WD Conversion Cargo

A-4, 5.3L, 8cyl	14	13/17	$3,700	2	Gas	430
	11	10/13	$4,150	2	E85	340

Express 1500 AWD Cargo

A-4, 5.3L, 8cyl	14	13/17	$3,700	2	Gas	430
	11	10/12	$4,150	3	E85	340

Express 1500 AWD Conversion Cargo

A-4, 5.3L, 8cyl	14	13/17	$3,700	2	Gas	430
	10	9/12	$4,550	2	E85	310

Express 2500 2WD Conversion Cargo MDPV

A-6, 6.0L, 8cyl	12	10/15	$4,300	1	Gas	370
	9	7/11	$5,050	1	E85	280

FORD

E150 Van FFV

A-4, 4.6L, 8cyl	15	13/16	$3,450	2	Gas	498
	11	10/12	$4,150	2	E85	365
A-4, 5.4L, 8cyl	14	12/16	$3,700	2	Gas	465
	10	9/12	$4,550	2	E85	332

E250 Van FFV

A-4, 4.6L, 8cyl	15	13/16	$3,450	2	Gas	498
	11	10/12	$4,150	2	E85	365
A-4, 5.4L, 8cyl	14	12/16	$3,700	2	Gas	465
	10	9/12	$4,550	2	E85	332

E350 Van FFV

A-4, 5.4L, 8cyl	13	12/16	$3,950	1	Gas	432
	10	9/12	$4,550	2	E85	332

GMC

Savana 1500 AWD (cargo)

A-4, 5.3L, 8cyl	14	13/17	$3,700	2	Gas	430
	11	10/12	$4,150	3	E85	340

Savana 1500 AWD Conversion (cargo)

A-4, 5.3L, 8cyl	14	13/17	$3,700	2	Gas	430
	10	9/12	$4,550	2	E85	310

Savana 1500 2WD (cargo)

A-4, 5.3L, 8cyl	15	13/18	$3,450	2	Gas	470
	11	10/13	$4,150	3	E85	340

Savana 1500 2WD Conversion (cargo)

A-4, 5.3L, 8cyl	14	13/17	$3,700	2	Gas	430
	11	10/13	$4,150	2	E85	340

Savana 2500 2WD Conversion (cargo) MDPV

A-6, 6.0L, 8cyl	12	10/15	$4,300	1	Gas	370
	9	7/11	$5,050	1	E85	280

VANS, PASSENGER TYPE

CHEVROLET

Express 1500 2WD Passenger

A-4, 5.3L, 8cyl	14	13/17	$3,700	2	Gas	430
	11	10/13	$4,150	2	E85	340

Express 1500 AWD Passenger

A-4, 5.3L, 8cyl	14	13/17	$3,700	2	Gas	430
	10	9/12	$4,550	2	E85	310

Express 2500 2WD Passenger MDPV

A-6, 6.0L, 8cyl	13	11/16	$3,950	1	Gas	400
	9	8/11	$5,050	1	E85	280

Express 3500 2WD Passenger MDPV

A-6, 6.0L, 8cyl	12	11/16	$4,300	1	Gas	370
	9	8/11	$5,050	1	E85	280

FORD

E150 Wagon FFV

A-4, 4.6L, 8cyl	14	13/16	$3,700	2	Gas	465
	10	9/12	$4,550	2	E85	332
A-4, 5.4L, 8cyl	13	12/16	$3,950	1	Gas	432
	10	9/12	$4,550	2	E85	332

E350 Wagon FFV

A-4, 5.4L, 8cyl	13	11/15	$3,950	1	Gas	432
	10	9/11	$4,550	2	E85	332

GMC

Savana 1500 2WD (Passenger)

A-4, 5.3L, 8cyl	14	13/17	$3,700	2	Gas	430
	11	10/13	$4,150	2	E85	340

Manufacturer Model Configuration (trans, eng size, cyl)	MPG Comb	MPG City/Hwy	Annual Fuel Cost	GHG Rating	Fuel	Range (miles)
Savana 1500 AWD (Passenger)						
A-4, 5.3L, 8cyl	14	13/17	$3,700	2	Gas	430
	10	9/12	$4,550	2	E85	310
Savana 2500 2WD (Passenger) MDPV						
A-6, 6.0L, 8cyl	13	11/16	$3,950	1	Gas	400
	9	8/11	$5,050	1	E85	280
Savana 3500 2WD (Passenger) MDPV						
A-6, 6.0L, 8cyl	12	11/16	$4,300	1	Gas	370
	9	8/11	$5,050	1	E85	280

MINIVANS 2WD

CHRYSLER
Town and Country

Manufacturer Model Configuration (trans, eng size, cyl)	MPG Comb	MPG City/Hwy	Annual Fuel Cost	GHG Rating	Fuel	Range (miles)
A-6, 3.6L, 6cyl	20	17/25	$2,600	5	Gas	400
	14	12/18	$3,250	5	E85	280

DODGE
Grand Caravan

A-6, 3.6L, 6cyl	20	17/25	$2,600	5	Gas	400
	14	12/18	$3,250	5	E85	280

RAM
C/V

A-6, 3.6L, 6cyl	21	18/26	$2,450	5	Gas	420
	15	13/18	$3,050	5	E85	300

VOLKSWAGEN
Routan

A-6, 3.6L, 6cyl	20	17/25	$2,600	5	Gas	400
	14	12/18	$3,250	5	E85	280

SMALL SPORT UTILITY VEHICLES 2WD

CHEVROLET
Captiva FWD

A-6, 2.4L, 4cyl	23	20/28	$2,250	6	Gas	380
	18	15/22	$2,550	6	E85	300
A-6, 3.0L, 6cyl	19	17/24	$2,700	4	Gas	370
	14	12/17	$3,250	5	E85	270

Equinox FWD

A-6, 2.4L, 4cyl	26	22/32	$2,000	7	Gas	490
	18	15/22	$2,550	6	E85	340
A-6, 3.6L, 6cyl	20	17/24	$2,600	5	Gas	420
	16	13/22	$2,850	6	E85	330

DODGE
Journey FWD

A-6, 3.6L, 6cyl	19	17/25	$2,700	4	Gas	390
	14	12/18	$3,250	5	E85	287

GMC
Terrain FWD

A-6, 2.4L, 4cyl	26	22/32	$2,000	7	Gas	490
	18	15/22	$2,550	6	E85	340
A-6, 3.6L, 6cyl	20	17/24	$2,600	5	Gas	420
	16	13/22	$2,850	6	E85	330

SMALL SPORT UTILITY VEHICLES 4WD

AUDI
Q5

A-S8, 2.0L, 4cyl	23	20/28	$2,450	6	P	455
	16	14/19	$2,850	6	E85	317

CHEVROLET
Captiva AWD

A-6, 3.0L, 6cyl	18	16/22	$2,850	4	Gas	300
	13	11/16	$3,500	4	E85	220

Equinox AWD

A-6, 2.4L, 4cyl	23	20/29	$2,250	6	Gas	430
	17	14/20	$2,700	6	E85	320
A-6, 3.6L, 6cyl	19	16/23	$2,700	4	Gas	400
	14	12/17	$3,250	5	E85	290

GMC
Terrain AWD

A-6, 2.4L, 4cyl	23	20/29	$2,250	6	Gas	430
	17	14/20	$2,700	6	E85	320
A-6, 3.6L, 6cyl	19	16/23	$2,700	4	Gas	400
	14	12/17	$3,250	5	E85	290

STANDARD SPORT UTILITY VEHICLES 2WD

CADILLAC
Escalade 2WD

A-6, 6.2L, 8cyl	16	14/18	$3,250	3	Gas	410
	12	10/15	$3,800	3	E85	310

Escalade ESV 2WD

A-6, 6.2L, 8cyl	16	14/18	$3,250	3	Gas	510
	12	10/15	$3,800	3	E85	380

CHEVROLET
Suburban C10 2WD

A-6, 5.3L, 8cyl	17	15/21	$3,050	3	Gas	540
	13	11/16	$3,500	4	E85	410

Tahoe C10 2WD

A-6, 5.3L, 8cyl	17	15/21	$3,050	3	Gas	430
	13	11/16	$3,500	4	E85	330

DODGE
Durango RWD

A-8, 3.6L, 6cyl	20	18/25	$2,600	5	Gas	494
	15	13/19	$3,050	5	E85	370

FORD
Expedition 2WD FFV

A-6, 5.4L, 8cyl	16	14/20	$3,250	3	Gas	448/536
	12	10/14	$3,800	3	E85	336/402

Explorer 2WD FFV

A-S6, 3.5L, 6cyl	20	17/24	$2,600	5	Gas	372
	15	13/18	$3,050	5	E85	279

GMC
Yukon C10 2WD

A-6, 5.3L, 8cyl	17	15/21	$3,050	3	Gas	430
	13	11/16	$3,500	4	E85	330
A-6, 6.2L, 8cyl	16	14/18	$3,250	3	Gas	410
	12	10/15	$3,800	3	E85	310

Yukon XL C10 2WD

A-6, 5.3L, 8cyl	17	15/21	$3,050	3	Gas	540
	13	11/16	$3,500	4	E85	410
A-6, 6.2L, 8cyl	16	14/18	$3,250	3	Gas	510
	12	10/15	$3,800	3	E85	380

Manufacturer Model Configuration (trans, eng size, cyl)	MPG Comb	City/Hwy	Annual Fuel Cost	GHG Rating	Fuel	Range (miles)
JEEP						
Grand Cherokee 2WD						
A-8, 3.6L, 6cyl	20	17/25	$2,600	5	Gas	469
	16	14/19	$2,850	5	E85	395
LINCOLN						
Navigator 2WD FFV						
A-6, 5.4L, 8cyl	16	14/20	$3,250	3	Gas	448/536
	12	10/14	$3,800	3	E85	336/402
NISSAN						
Armada 2WD						
A-5, 5.6L, 8cyl	15	12/19	$3,450	2	Gas	420
	11	9/13	$4,150	2	E85	310

STANDARD SPORT UTILITY VEHICLES 4WD

Manufacturer Model Configuration (trans, eng size, cyl)	MPG Comb	City/Hwy	Annual Fuel Cost	GHG Rating	Fuel	Range (miles)
CADILLAC						
Escalade AWD						
A-6, 6.2L, 8cyl	15	13/18	$3,450	2	Gas	380
	12	10/14	$3,800	3	E85	310
Escalade ESV AWD						
A-6, 6.2L, 8cyl	14	13/18	$3,700	2	Gas	450
	10	9/13	$4,550	2	E85	320
CHEVROLET						
Suburban K10 4WD						
A-6, 5.3L, 8cyl	17	15/21	$3,050	3	Gas	540
	13	11/16	$3,500	4	E85	410
Tahoe K10 4WD						
A-6, 5.3L, 8cyl	17	15/21	$3,050	3	Gas	430
	13	11/16	$3,500	4	E85	330
DODGE						
Durango AWD						
A-8, 3.6L, 6cyl	19	17/24	$2,700	4	Gas	469
	15	13/18	$3,050	5	E85	370
FORD						
Expedition 4WD FFV						
A-6, 5.4L, 8cyl	15	13/18	$3,450	2	Gas	420/502
	11	9/13	$4,150	2	E85	308/368
Explorer AWD FFV						
A-S6, 3.5L, 6cyl	19	17/23	$2,700	4	Gas	353
	14	12/17	$3,250	5	E85	260
GMC						
Yukon Denali K10 AWD						
A-6, 6.2L, 8cyl	15	13/18	$3,450	2	Gas	380
	12	10/14	$3,800	3	E85	310
Yukon K10 4WD						
A-6, 5.3L, 8cyl	17	15/21	$3,050	3	Gas	430
	13	11/16	$3,500	4	E85	330
Yukon XL K10 4WD						
A-6, 5.3L, 8cyl	17	15/21	$3,050	3	Gas	540
	13	11/16	$3,500	4	E85	410
Yukon XL K10 AWD						
A-6, 6.2L, 8cyl	14	13/18	$3,700	2	Gas	450
	10	9/13	$4,550	2	E85	320
JEEP						
Grand Cherokee 4WD						
A-8, 3.6L, 6cyl	19	17/24	$2,700	4	Gas	469
	15	13/18	$3,050	5	E85	370
LAND ROVER						
Range Rover FFV						
A-S8, 3.0L, 6cyl	19	17/23	$3,000	4	P	526
	14	12/16	$3,250	4	E85	388
A-S8, 5.0L, 8cyl	16	14/19	$3,550	3	P	443
	11	9/14	$4,150	3	E85	305
Range Rover L FFV						
A-S8, 3.0L, 6cyl	19	17/23	$3,000	4	P	526
	14	12/16	$3,250	4	E85	388
A-S8, 5.0L, 8cyl	16	14/19	$3,550	3	P	443
	11	9/14	$4,150	3	E85	305
Range Rover Sport FFV						
A-S8, 3.0L, 6cyl	19	17/23	$3,000	4	P	526
	14	12/16	$3,250	4	E85	388
A-S8, 5.0L, 8cyl	16	14/19	$3,550	3	P	443
	11	10/14	$4,150	3	E85	305
LINCOLN						
Navigator 4WD FFV						
A-6, 5.4L, 8cyl	15	13/18	$3,450	2	Gas	420/502
	11	9/13	$4,150	2	E85	308/368
MERCEDES-BENZ						
ML350 4matic						
A-7, 3.5L, 6cyl	19	17/22	$3,000	4	P	470
	15	13/17	$3,050	5	E85	370
NISSAN						
Armada 4WD						
A-5, 5.6L, 8cyl	14	12/18	$3,700	2	Gas	390
	11	9/13	$4,150	2	E85	310
TOYOTA						
Sequoia 4WD FFV						
A-S6, 5.7L, 8cyl	14	13/17	$3,700	2	Gas	370
	10	9/12	$4,550	2	E85	264

Interior Volume (cu.ft.) — Passenger / Cargo

	2dr	4dr	Hatch	Pg
Spark EV		86/11		5,9,33
SS		112/17		17
Suburban C10 2WD				26,40
Suburban K10 4WD				27,41
Tahoe C10 2WD				26,40
Tahoe K10 4WD				27,41
Traverse AWD				27
Traverse FWD				26
Volt			90/18	11,34
CHRYSLER				
200		100/14		14,37
200 Convertible	88/13			11,37
300		106/16		17,38
300 AWD		106/16		17,38
300 SRT8		106/16		17
Town and Country				22,40
DODGE				
Avenger		100/13		14,37
Challenger	94/16			14
Challenger SRT8	94/16			14
Charger		105/16		18,38
Charger AWD		105/16		18,38
Charger SRT8		105/16		18
Dart			97/13	14,37
Dart Aero			97/13	14
Dart GT			97/13	14
Durango AWD				27,41
Durango RWD				26,40
Grand Caravan				22,40
Journey AWD				25
Journey FWD				23,40
FERRARI				
458 Italia				6
458 Spider				6
California	75/7			7
F12				6
FF			90/22	14
FIAT				
500		76/7		7
500 Abarth		76/7		8
500 L	100/21			19
500e			72/7	5,8,33
FORD				
C-MAX Energi Plug-in Hybrid		100/19		5,14,34
C-MAX Hybrid FWD		100/24		5,18,36
E150 Van FFV				21,39
E150 Wagon FFV				5,22,39
E250 Van FFV				21,39
E350 Van				21
E350 Van FFV				21,39
E350 Wagon				22
E350 Wagon FFV				22,39
Edge AWD				25
Edge FWD				23
Escape AWD				25
Escape FWD				23
Expedition 2WD FFV				26,40
Expedition 4WD FFV				27,41
Explorer 2WD FFV				26,40
Explorer AWD				28
Explorer AWD FFV				28,41
Explorer FWD				26
F150 Pickup 2WD				20
F150 Pickup 2WD FFV				20,38

Interior Volume (cu.ft.) — Passenger / Cargo

	2dr	4dr	Hatch	Pg
F150 Pickup 4WD				20
F150 Pickup 4WD FFV				21,39
F150 Raptor Pickup 4WD				21
Fiesta FWD	85/12		85/15	9
Fiesta SFE FWD	85/12		85/15	5,9
Fiesta ST FWD			85/15	11
Flex AWD				28
Flex FWD				26
Focus Electric	90/13		90/23	5,11,33
Focus FWD	90/13		90/23	11
Focus FWD FFV	90/13		90/23	11,37
Focus SFE FWD FFV	90/13		90/23	11,37
Fusion AWD		100/16		14
Fusion Energi Plug-in Hybrid		103/8		5,15,34
Fusion FWD		100/16		15
Fusion Hybrid FWD		101/16		15,35
Mustang	83/13			9
Mustang Convertible	81/9			9
Special Service Police FWD		103/17		18
Taurus AWD		102/20		18
Taurus AWD FFV		102/20		18,38
Taurus FWD		102/20		18
Taurus FWD FFV		102/20		18,38
Transit Connect Van 2WD				5,22
Transit Connect Wagon FWD				5,22
Transit Connect Wagon LWB FWD				22
GMC				
Acadia AWD				28
Acadia FWD				27
Savana 1500 AWD (cargo)				21,39
Savana 1500 AWD Conversion (cargo)				21,39
Savana 1500 2WD (cargo)				5,21,39
Savana 1500 2WD (Passenger)				5,22,39
Savana 1500 2WD Conversion (cargo)				22,39
Savana 1500 AWD (Passenger)				5,22,40
Savana 2500 2WD (Passenger) MDPV				22,40
Savana 2500 2WD Conversion (cargo) MDPV				22,39
Savana 3500 2WD (Passenger) MDPV				22,40
Sierra C15 2WD				20,38
Sierra K15 4WD				21,39
Terrain AWD				25,40
Terrain FWD		100/28		23,40
Yukon C10 2WD				27,40
Yukon Denali K10 AWD				28,41
Yukon K10 4WD				28,41
Yukon XL C10 2WD				27,40
Yukon XL K10 4WD				28,41
Yukon XL K10 AWD				28,41
HONDA				
Accord	92/14	103/16		15
Accord Hybrid	92/14	103/16		15,35
Accord Plug-in Hybrid		103/9		15,34
Civic Hybrid		95/11		11,35
Civic Natural Gas		95/6		11,32
CR-V 2WD				23
CR-V 4WD				25
CR-Z				5,6,35
Crosstour 2WD				23
Crosstour 4WD				25
FCX Clarity				32
Fit EV	91/21			5,19,33
Insight	85/16			11,35
Odyssey				22
Pilot 2WD				23

Interior Volume (cu.ft.) — Passenger / Cargo

	2dr	4dr	Hatch	Pg
Pilot 4WD				25
Ridgeline Truck 4WD				21
HYUNDAI				
Accent		90/14	90/19	11
Azera		106/16		18
Elantra		96/15		15
Elantra Coupe	95/15			15
Elantra GT			96/23	15
Elantra Limited		96/15		15
Equus		111/16		18
Genesis		109/16		18
Genesis Coupe	89/10			9
Genesis R Spec		109/16		18
Santa Fe 2WD				23
Santa Fe 4WD				25
Santa Fe Sport 2WD				23
Santa Fe Sport 4WD				25
Sonata		104/16		18
Sonata Hybrid		104/12		15,35
Sonata Hybrid Limited		104/12		15,35
Tucson 2WD				23
Tucson 4WD				25
Veloster		90/16		11
INFINITI				
Q50		100/14		15
Q50 AWD		100/14		15
Q50 Hybrid		100/9		11,35
Q50 Hybrid AWD		100/9		11,35
Q50a		102/14		15
Q50a AWD		102/14		15
Q50S Hybrid		100/9		11,35
Q50S Hybrid AWD		100/9		11,35
Q60 AWD Coupe	85/7			9
Q60 Convertible	78/10			9
Q60 Coupe	85/7			9
Q70		104/15		15
Q70 AWD		104/15		15
Q70 Hybrid		104/11		15,35
QX50		92/19		19
QX50 AWD		92/19		19
QX60 AWD				25
QX60 FWD				23
QX60 Hybrid AWD				28,36
QX60 Hybrid FWD				27,36
QX70 AWD				25
QX70 RWD				23
QX80 2WD				27
QX80 4WD				28
JAGUAR				
F-Type Convertible	64/8			6
F-Type S Convertible	64/8			6
F-Type V8 S Convertible	64/8			6
XF		95/18		15
XF AWD		95/18		15
XF FFV		95/18		15,38
XJ		102/18		18
XJ AWD		102/18		18
XJ FFV		102/18		18,38
XJL		109/18		18
XJL AWD		109/18		18
XJL FFV		109/18		18,38
XK	74/10			8
XK Convertible	74/10			8

Interior Volume (cu.ft.)
Passenger / Cargo

	2dr	4dr	Hatch	Pg
JEEP				
Cherokee 4WD				25
Cherokee 4WD Active Drive II				25
Cherokee FWD				23
Cherokee Trailhawk 4WD				25
Compass 4WD				25
Compass FWD				23
Grand Cherokee 2WD				27,30,41
Grand Cherokee 4WD				28,31,41
Grand Cherokee SRT8				28
Patriot 4WD				25
Patriot FWD				24
Wrangler 4WD				25
Wrangler Unlimited 4WD				25
KIA				
Cadenza		106/15		18
Forte		96/14		15
Forte 5			98/23	18
Forte Eco		96/14		15
Forte Koup	92/13			11
Optima		102/15		15
Optima Hybrid		102/11		15,35
Optima Hybrid EX		102/11		15,35
Rio		88/14	89/15	11
Rio Eco		88/14	89/15	11
Sedona				22
Sorento 2WD				24
Sorento 4WD				25
Soul		101/24		19
Soul ECO dynamics		101/24		19
Sportage 2WD				24
Sportage 4WD				25
LAMBORGHINI				
Aventador Coupe				6
Aventador Roadster				6
Aventador Veneno Coupe				6
Gallardo Coupe				7
Gallardo Spyder				7
LAND ROVER				
LR2				25
LR4				28
Range Rover				28
Range Rover Evoque				25
Range Rover FFV				28,41
Range Rover L FFV				28,41
Range Rover Sport				28
Range Rover Sport FFV				28,41
LEXUS				
CT 200h			86/14	12,35
ES 300h		100/12		15,35
ES 350		100/15		15
GS 350		99/14		15
GS 350 AWD		99/14		15
GS 450h		99/13		15,35
GX 460				28
IS 250		90/11		12
IS 250 AWD		90/11		12
IS 250 C	77/11			9
IS 350		90/11		12
IS 350 AWD		90/11		12
IS 350 C	77/11			9
IS F		88/11		9
LS 460		103/14		15
LS 460 AWD		103/14		15
LS 460 L		102/14		15
LS 460 L AWD		102/14		15
LS 600h L		102/10		15,35

Interior Volume (cu.ft.)
Passenger / Cargo

	2dr	4dr	Hatch	Pg
LX 570				28
RX 350				24
RX 350 AWD				25
RX 450h				24,36
RX 450h AWD				25,36
LINCOLN				
MKS AWD		105/18		18
MKS FWD		105/18		18
MKT AWD				25
MKT FWD				27
MKT Livery AWD				22
MKT Livery FWD				22
MKX AWD				25
MKX FWD				24
MKZ AWD		99/16		16
MKZ FWD		99/16		16
MKZ Hybrid FWD		99/12		16,36
Navigator 2WD FFV				27,41
Navigator 4WD FFV				28,41
LOTUS				
Evora	48/2	48/2		8
MASERATI				
Ghibli V6		108/10		16
Ghibli V6 AWD		108/10		16
GranTurismo	86/6			9
GranTurismo Convertible	85/5			9
Quattroporte GTS		114/19		18
Quattroporte SQ4 V6		114/19		18
MAZDA				
2			87/13	12
3 4-Door		96/12		12
3 5-Door			96/22	16
5				5,23
6		100/15		16
CX-5 2WD				24
CX-5 4WD				25
CX-9 2WD				24
CX-9 4WD				25
MX-5				7
MCLAREN				
P1				34
MERCEDES-BENZ				
C250		88/12		12
C250 Coupe	81/12			9
C300 4matic		88/12		12,37
C350		88/12		12,37
C350 4matic Coupe	81/12			9
C350 Coupe	81/12			9
C63 AMG		88/12		12
C63 AMG Coupe	81/12			9
CL550 4matic	91/14			12
CL600	91/14			12
CL63 AMG	91/14			12
CL65 AMG	91/14			12
CLA250		88/13		12
CLA45 AMG 4matic	88/13			12
CLS550		92/11		12
CLS550 4matic		92/11		12
CLS63 AMG		92/11		12
CLS63 AMG 4matic		92/11		12
CLS63 AMG S		92/11		12
CLS63 AMG S 4matic		92/11		12
E250 Bluetec		98/13		16,30
E250 Bluetec 4matic		98/13		16,30
E350		98/13		16,38

Interior Volume (cu.ft.)
Passenger / Cargo

	2dr	4dr	Hatch	Pg
E350 4matic		98/13		16,38
E350 4matic (wagon)		100/36		19
E350 4matic Coupe	81/11			9,37
E350 Convertible	80/6			9,37
E350 Coupe	81/11			10,37
E400 Hybrid		98/13		16,36
E550 4matic		98/13		16
E550 Convertible	80/6			10
E550 Coupe	81/11			10
E63 AMG		98/13		16
E63 AMG 4matic		98/13		16
E63 AMG 4matic (wagon)		100/36		19
E63 AMG S		98/13		16
E63 AMG S 4matic		98/13		16
E63 AMG S 4matic (wagon)		100/36		19
G550				28
G63 AMG				28
GL350 Bluetec 4matic				28,31
GL450 4matic				28
GL550 4matic				28
GL63 AMG				28
GLK250 Bluetec 4matic				25,30
GLK350				24
GLK350 4matic				26
ML350				27
ML350 4matic				28,41
ML350 Bluetec 4matic				28,31
ML550 4matic				28
ML63 AMG				28
S550		112/12		18
S550 4matic		112/12		18
S63 AMG 4matic		112/12		18
SL550				7
SL63 AMG				7
SL65 AMG				7
SLK250				7
SLK350				7
SLK55 AMG				7
SLS AMG Black Series Coupe				7
SLS AMG Coupe				7
SLS AMG GT Coupe				7
SLS AMG GT Roadster				7
SLS AMG Roadster				7
MINI				
Cooper Clubman			80/9	10
Cooper Clubvan				7
Cooper Convertible	72/6			8
Cooper Countryman			87/16	12
Cooper Coupe				7
Cooper Paceman			87/14	12
Cooper Roadster				7
Cooper S Clubman			80/9	10
Cooper S Convertible	72/6			8
Cooper S Countryman			87/16	12
Cooper S Countryman All4			87/16	12
Cooper S Coupe				7
Cooper S Paceman			87/14	12
Cooper S Paceman All4			87/14	12
Cooper S Roadster				7
JCW Countryman All4			87/16	12
JCW Paceman All4			87/14	12
John Cooper Works Clubman			80/9	10
John Cooper Works Convertible	72/6			8
John Cooper Works Coupe				7
John Cooper Works Roadster				7

MITSUBISHI

	2dr	4dr	Hatch	Pg
Lancer		93/12		12
Lancer AWD		93/12		12
Lancer Evolution		93/7		12
Lancer Sportback		95/14		19
Mirage		86/17	86/17	12
Outlander 2WD		128/10		24
Outlander 4WD		128/10		26
Outlander Sport 2WD		97/22		24
Outlander Sport 4WD		97/22		26

NISSAN

	2dr	4dr	Hatch	Pg
370Z	52/7			7
370Z Roadster	52/4			7
Altima		102/15		16
Armada 2WD				27,41
Armada 4WD				29,41
Cube		98/11		19
Frontier 2WD				20
Frontier 4WD				20
GT-R	79/9			10
Juke		87/10		19
Juke AWD		87/10		19
Leaf			92/24	5,16,33
Maxima		96/14		16
Murano AWD				26
Murano CrossCabriolet				26
Murano FWD				24
NV200 Cargo Van				22
Pathfinder 2WD				24
Pathfinder 4WD				26
Pathfinder Hybrid 2WD				27,36
Pathfinder Hybrid 4WD				29,36
Quest				23
Rogue AWD				26
Rogue FWD				24
Rogue Select AWD				26
Rogue Select FWD				24
Sentra		96/15		16
Sentra FE		96/15		16
Titan 2WD				20,38
Titan 4WD				21,39
Versa		90/15	94/19	12
Xterra 2WD				24
Xterra 4WD				26

PORSCHE

	2dr	4dr	Hatch	Pg
911 Carrera	70/5			8
911 Carrera 4	70/5			8
911 Carrera 4 Cabriolet	68/5			8
911 Carrera 4S	70/5			8
911 Carrera 4S Cabriolet	68/5			8
911 Carrera Cabriolet	68/5			8
911 Carrera S	70/5			8
911 Carrera S Cabriolet	68/5			8
911 GT3				7
911 Targa 4	70/5			8
911 Targa 4S	70/5			8
911 Turbo	70/5			8
911 Turbo Cabriolet	68/5			8
911 Turbo S	70/5			8
911 Turbo S Cabriolet	70/5			8
Boxster				7
Boxster S				7
Cayenne				29
Cayenne Diesel				29,31

	2dr	4dr	Hatch	Pg
Cayenne GTS				29
Cayenne S				29
Cayenne S Hybrid				29,36
Cayenne Turbo				29
Cayenne Turbo S				29
Cayman				7
Cayman S				7
Panamera		108/16		18
Panamera 4		108/16		18
Panamera 4S		108/16		18
Panamera 4S Executive		108/16		18
Panamera GTS		108/16		18
Panamera S		108/16		19
Panamera S E-Hybrid				34
Panamera Turbo		108/16		19
Panamera Turbo Executive		108/16		19
Panamera Turbo S		108/16		19
Panamera Turbo S Executive		108/16		19

RAM

	2dr	4dr	Hatch	Pg
1500 2WD				5,20,30,38
1500 4WD				21,30,39
1500 HFE 2WD				20
C/V				23,40

ROLLS-ROYCE

	2dr	4dr	Hatch	Pg
Ghost		111/14		19
Ghost EWB		117/14		19
Phantom		113/14		19
Phantom Coupe	96/13			12
Phantom Drophead Coupe	97/11			13
Phantom EWB		125/14		19
Wraith	99/13			16

ROUSH PERFORMANCE

	2dr	4dr	Hatch	Pg
F150 Pickup 2WD				20
F150 Pickup 4WD				21
F150 Raptor Pickup 4WD				21
Stage 3 Mustang	83/13			10

SCION

	2dr	4dr	Hatch	Pg
FR-S	77/7			8
iQ		74/4		5,8
tC		90/15		13
xB	101/22			19
xD		84/11		10

SMART

	2dr	4dr	Hatch	Pg
fortwo cabriolet				7
fortwo coupe				7
fortwo electric drive convertible				5,7,33
fortwo electric drive coupe				5,7,33

SRT

	2dr	4dr	Hatch	Pg
Viper				7

SUBARU

	2dr	4dr	Hatch	Pg
BRZ	77/7			8
Forester AWD				26
Impreza AWD		96/12		13
Impreza Wagon AWD		98/23		19
Legacy AWD		103/15		16
Outback AWD				26
Tribeca AWD				26
XV Crosstrek AWD				26
XV Crosstrek Hybrid AWD				5,26,36

TESLA

	2dr	4dr	Hatch	Pg
Model S (60 kWh battery pack)				33
Model S (85 kWh battery pack)				33

TOYOTA

	2dr	4dr	Hatch	Pg
4Runner 2WD				27
4Runner 4WD				29
Avalon		104/16		16
Avalon Hybrid		104/14		16,36
Camry		103/15		16
Camry Hybrid LE		103/13		16,36
Camry Hybrid XLE/SE		103/13		16,36
Corolla		98/13		16
Corolla LE Eco		98/13		16
FJ Cruiser 2WD				24
FJ Cruiser 4WD				26
Highlander 2WD				24
Highlander AWD				29
Highlander Hybrid 4WD				5,29,36
Highlander Hybrid 4WD LE Plus				5,29,36
Land Cruiser Wagon 4WD				29
Prius		94/22		5,16,36
Prius c		87/17		5,13,35
Prius Plug-in Hybrid		94/22		5,16,34
Prius v		97/34		5,19,36
RAV4				24
RAV4 AWD				26
RAV4 EV				5,24,33
RAV4 Limited AWD				26
Sequoia 2WD				27
Sequoia 4WD				29
Sequoia 4WD FFV				29,41
Sienna 2WD				23
Sienna AWD				23
Tacoma 2WD				5,20
Tacoma 4WD				20
Tundra 2WD				20
Tundra 4WD				21
Tundra 4WD FFV				21,39
Venza				24
Venza 4WD				26
Yaris			85/15	13

VOLKSWAGEN

	2dr	4dr	Hatch	Pg
Beetle			85/15	13,30
Beetle Convertible	81/7			10,30
CC	94/13			13
CC 4motion	94/13			13
Eos	77/11			10
Golf			94/15	13,30
GTI			94/15	13
Jetta		94/16		13,30
Jetta Hybrid		94/16		13,35
Jetta SportWagen		92/33		19,30
Passat		102/16		17,30
Routan				23,40
Tiguan				24
Tiguan 4motion				26
Touareg				29,31
Touareg Hybrid				29,36

VOLVO

	2dr	4dr	Hatch	Pg
S60 AWD		92/14		13
S60 FWD		92/14		13
S80 AWD		98/15		17
S80 FWD		98/15		17
XC60 AWD				26
XC60 FWD		99/34		24
XC70 AWD				26
XC70 FWD		98/37		24
XC90 AWD				29
XC90 FWD				27

US Government Printing Office
Laurel Publications Distribution Center
c/o Fuel Economy Guide
8660 Cherry Lane
Laurel, MD 20707

GETTING TO KNOW THE NEW FUEL ECONOMY AND ENVIRONMENT LABEL

EPA recently redesigned the Fuel Economy and Environment labels that must be affixed to new vehicles starting with the 2013 model year. The example below shows a sample label for a gasoline vehicle. Slightly different designs are used for flexible-fuel vehicles, electric vehicles, and plug-in hybrids. For more in-depth descriptions of label information for all vehicle types, visit **www.fueleconomy.gov**

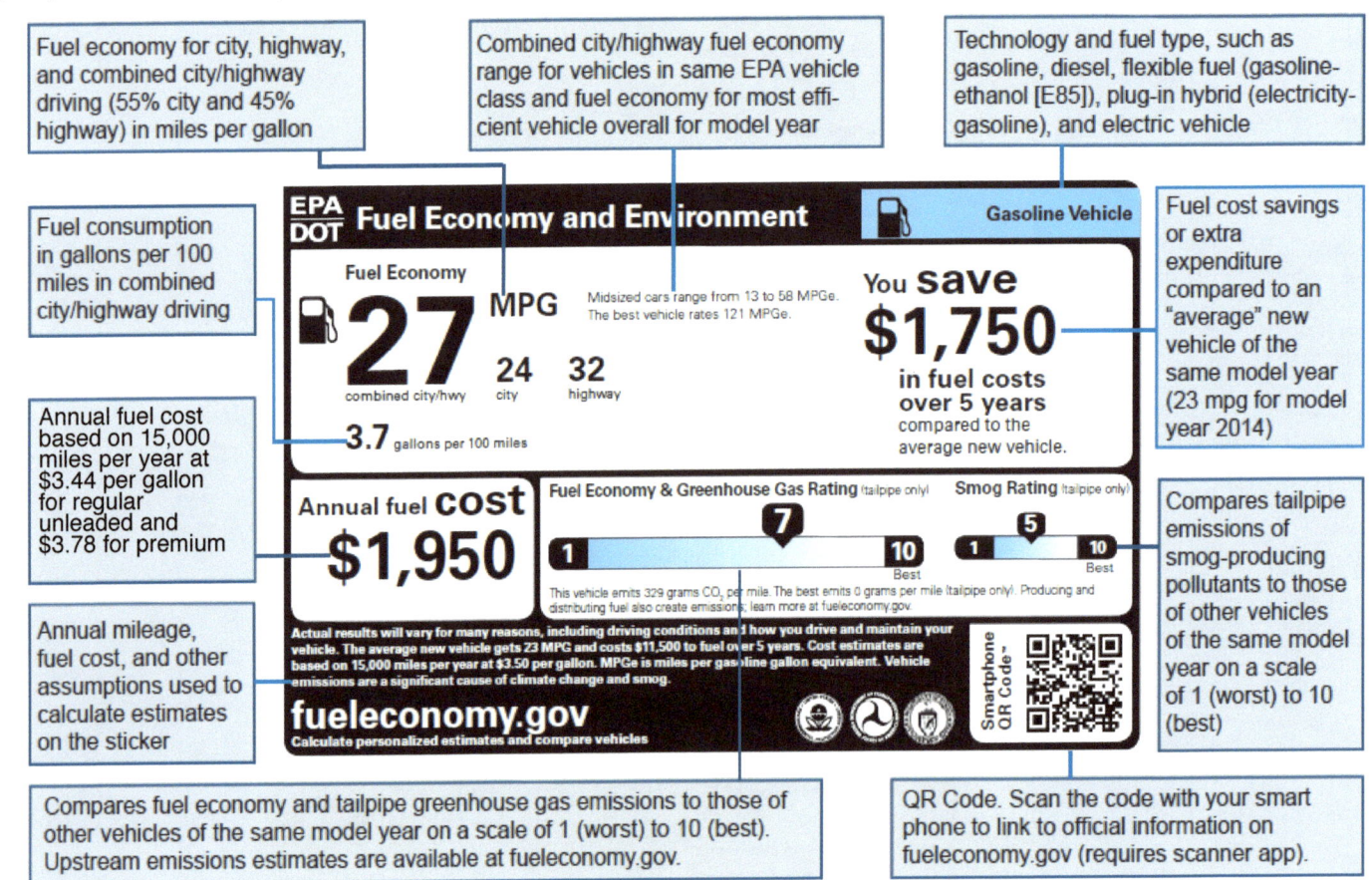

Fuel economy for city, highway, and combined city/highway driving (55% city and 45% highway) in miles per gallon

Combined city/highway fuel economy range for vehicles in same EPA vehicle class and fuel economy for most efficient vehicle overall for model year

Technology and fuel type, such as gasoline, diesel, flexible fuel (gasoline-ethanol [E85]), plug-in hybrid (electricity-gasoline), and electric vehicle

Fuel consumption in gallons per 100 miles in combined city/highway driving

Fuel cost savings or extra expenditure compared to an "average" new vehicle of the same model year (23 mpg for model year 2014)

Annual fuel cost based on 15,000 miles per year at $3.44 per gallon for regular unleaded and $3.78 for premium

Compares tailpipe emissions of smog-producing pollutants to those of other vehicles of the same model year on a scale of 1 (worst) to 10 (best)

Annual mileage, fuel cost, and other assumptions used to calculate estimates on the sticker

Compares fuel economy and tailpipe greenhouse gas emissions to those of other vehicles of the same model year on a scale of 1 (worst) to 10 (best). Upstream emissions estimates are available at fueleconomy.gov.

QR Code. Scan the code with your smart phone to link to official information on fueleconomy.gov (requires scanner app).

www.ingramcontent.com/pod-product-compliance
Lightning Source LLC
Chambersburg PA
CBHW041518280526

45792CB00004B/1294